North Wales Branch Line Album

Front cover: It must have been raining when this train left Builth for the storm sheet to be still above the footplate; or maybe they were expecting to run back into the bad weather down at Brecon. These storm sheets were unhandy contraptions held taut by heavy coil springs. They were hard to stretch and hook over the stanchions and they were apt to snap. At best this resulted in flapping chaos and at worst one of the crew got a clout over the head.

WR No 844, once Cambrian 0-6-0 Jones goods No 15 on a local train from Builth to Brecon caught near Three Cocks at 2pm on 2 May 1953. *J. F. Russell-Smith*

Back cover, top: L&NW Webb 2-4-2T No 465 now L&MR No 46604 leaving Rhyl with a train for Denbigh. The cracked and distorted smokebox door recalls the frequency at which L&NWR engines were seen 'on fire at both ends'. The 'quality' of the coal often given to the unfortunate crews resulted in accumulations of glowing half-burnt cinders and ash in the smokeboxes and the author remembers well seeing the red glowing half moons down the tunnel as Webb and Whale engines approached the platforms at New Street, Birmingham.
A. B. Crompton

Back cover, bottom: Great Central 0-6-2T now L&NE No 9340 waiting in Wrexham on the Cambrian line to take a substantial train to Chester 13 March 1948.
W. A. Camwell

North Wales Branch Line Album

C.C.Green MBE

LONDON

IAN ALLAN LTD

Dedication

To the miners and quarrymen of North Wales who set a standard of toil not likely to be equalled anywhere today. It was their application and skills in winning the raw materials from the mountains that called into being nearly every railway line mentioned in this book.

Cyflwyniad

I fwyngloddwyr a chwarelwyr Gogledd Cymru a osododd safon o lafurio y byddai'n anodd gweld ei thebyg yn unman heddiw. Eu hymroddiad a'u medr hwy yn ennill y defnyddiau crai o'r mynyddoedd a ddug i fodolaeth bron bob rheilffordd a enwir yn y llyfr hwn.

Readers will appreciate that this book was first published more than 10 years ago and that comments regarding preservation in North Wales that were contemporary when the book was first published are now historic. All the preserved railways mentioned have progressed well. The Cambrian Railways Society expects to be running trains in 1996: the Llangollen Railway Society offers a 5¼ mile run to Glyndyfrdwy and is about to extend another two miles: and the Vale of Rheidol is now owned by the Phyllis Rampton Narrow Gauge Railway Trust by whom the track and rolling stock have been much improved.

First published 1983
Reprinted 1996

ISBN 0 7110 1252 0

Published by Ian Allan Ltd, Shepperton, Surrey; and printed by Ian Allan Printing Ltd at their works at Coombelands in Runnymede, England.

It has been a conscious decision to include in this volume photographs of historic interest which might, in other conditions, have been excluded on grounds of quality. It is hoped that the reader will accept the consequent reduction in the production standards of some plates.

Contents

Introduction 6

Maps 8

The Forerunners 12

The Cambrian Branches 14

The Great Central Branches 27

The Great Western Branches 36

The London & North Western
   Branches from the Coast 50
   Branches across Clwyd 63

The Industrial Branches 69

The Industrial Railway Horse 78

The Manchester & Milford 80

The Narrow Gauge Branches 84

Railway Buses 106

Preservation 108

Introduction

In these islands the term branchline usually brings to mind a sleepy offshoot winding through gentle scenery to a little town out in the countryside. Traffic would have been entirely local and most of the goods would have flowed inwards, lime, fertilisers and feeding stuffs for the farmers and coal for the householders. Only passengers would have journeyed outwards: people going to shop in a larger market town and later on people commuting to work there; and all returning towards the end of the branch at the close of the day.

The branch lines of North Wales were of stronger and much more vigorous stuff, their reasons for being were minerals urgently needed elsewhere. A surprisingly large number of them were initially horse-drawn tramways, some pre-dating the steam-hauled railways by more than 40 years. A rare few had run their independant way to the River Dee some 90 years before 'big business' with all its wheeling and dealing had managed to project modern transport into the Welsh mountains.

Although frustrated initially by the Gauge Commission's ruling in 1846 that the 7ft gauge should not be allowed to develop beyond its existing trackage the Great Western Railway Company was the first big company to get into the field. By much boardroom manoeuvering it gathered in three standard-gauge companies which gave it a south to north route into the eastern flank of the area. These were the Chester & Birkenhead (later made into a joint line), the North Wales Mineral and the Shrewsbury, Oswestry & Chester Junction Railways. It narrowly missed a grab for the Chester & Holyhead Railway which had opened as far as Bangor by 1847 and which could have been an adequate substitute for the forbidden broad gauge line to Porth Dinllaen and the traffic with Northern Ireland. However the London & Birmingham/London & North Western's spies had detected the move in time and the Chester & Holyhead stayed in the clutches of Euston.

Further south the Cambrian's delicate skein of little companies was nearly 20 years behind.

The ambitions of Edward Watkin, the hard-headed Mancunian chairman of the Manchester, Sheffield & Lincolnshire, to gain control of a north to south direct route cutting across inside the rival companies' lines led him to foster the Welsh Railway Union by supporting the formation of any local line which could form a link. As financial problems (often fostered maliciously) developed he would have been ready with his hands cupped. Alas for devious scheming his connections got only as far as Wrexham; but he did get his company into the most profitable area at the north end; albeit after his term in office.

Many branchline companies formed in anticipation of main line construction were working almost as soon as the main had been driven past the valleys they were to serve;

but the Great Western/London & North Western/Great Central rivalries were to bring about some highly interesting developments at later dates.

From the first onset your publisher had indicated that the book should be one in which the narrow gauge was to be included along with the standard. Researches into literature and in the field have convinced your author that the early tramways and the industrial lines were also of much importance. To be observed as well was the fact that the whole area was a microcosm of all types of industrial development which had occurred elsewhere in these islands and that it could be taken as a modeller's shop window from which almost any style of prototype could be selected. After this the book just moulded itself inevitably into a summary of all forms and periods of rail-borne transport.

Acknowledgements

Photographs have been credited as far back as possible to the photographer where known, or to an appropriate body, or to the donor. Much help by way of conversation or correspondence was very kindly given by Dr B. S. Benedict; James Bentley; J. I. C. Boyd; V. Bradley; John Burman; W. A. Camwell; R. S. Carpenter; D. C. Carrington; Geoffrey Charles; George Dow; Colin Fry; P. J. Garland; Sir William Gladstone; E. W. Hannan; F. E. Hemming; S. H. P. Higgins; Philip G. Hindley; Owen Jenkins; M. E. M. Lloyd; N. R. Miller; R. W. Miller; J. Osbaldeston; Fred Orsler; J. W. Owen; O. H. Owen; L. W. Perkins; P. H. Pike; G. H. Platt; R. M. Platt; J. P. Richards; R. C. Riley; Major J. H. Sharpley; The Southern Counties Heavy Horse Association; T. E. Taylor; R. T. Taylor; Eric Thomas; E. S. Tonks; Oliver Veltom; B. S. Walker; L. Ward; Dr P. H. Whittaker; D. E. Yates; J. Hooson.

I never cease to marvel at the patience of and the courteous help given by Archivists, Librarians and their staffs and notably at: Birmingham University; City of Birmingham; Clwyd Record Offices; Gwynedd Archives Service; The National Library of Wales; Powys County Library, Newtown.

Much help too has come from British Rail at all levels.

For reading the proofs I am most grateful to Messrs E. W. Hannan and W. F. B. Price.

Left: Where railways began, — rail-guided manpower. Methusalem Jones was working slate at Diphwys by 1755 and soon others followed. Their internal systems will have been the first tramways in North-West Wales. This typical scene was taken at the Diphwys Casson c1885. Note the two men clasping arms about shoulders as they struggle to breast the heavy truck into the tunnel leading to the mill. *Clwyd Record Office*

7

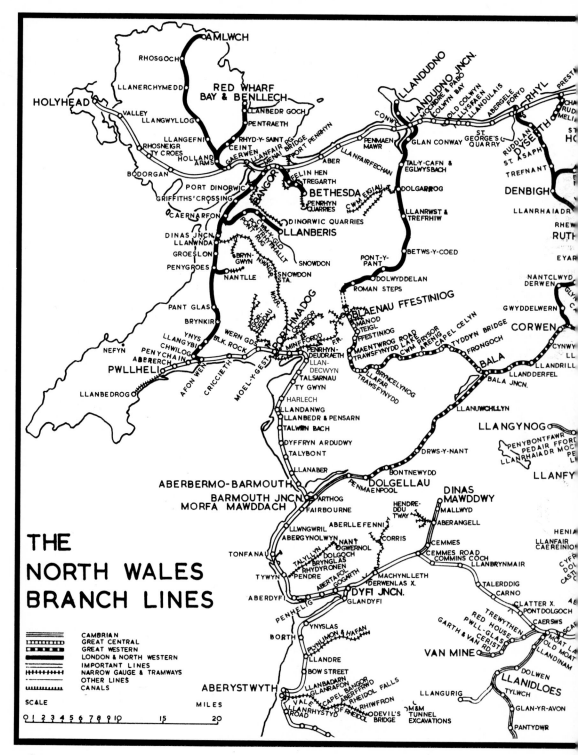

THE
NORTH WALES
BRANCH LINES

CAMBRIAN
GREAT CENTRAL
GREAT WESTERN
LONDON & NORTH WESTERN
IMPORTANT LINES
NARROW GAUGE & TRAMWAYS
OTHER LINES
CANALS

SCALE

MILES

0 1 2 3 4 5 6 7 8 9 10   15   20

8

Significant events which led railways into North Wales

A 1 October 1840. The Chester & Crewe Railway opened. Vested already in the Grand Junction Railway it went to the L&NWR.

B 1 March 1845. The Chester & Holyhead Railway started to grow westwards. It too went to the L&NWR.

C 4 July 1846. The North Wales Mineral Railway opened between Saltney and Ruabon. Later it was bought up by the GWR.

D 12 October 1848. The Shrewsbury & Chester Railway opened. This too was bought up by the GWR.

E 1 September 1854. Opening of the Shrewsbury & Birmingham by the GWR.

F 1 September 1858. The L&NWR opened Crewe to Shrewsbury.

G 27 January 1862. Opening of the GWR/L&NWR joint line from Shrewsbury to Buttington Junction on the Cambrian.

H 31 March 1890. Opening of the Chester & Connah's Quay Railway by the MS&L/GCR management.

I 18 May 1896. Opening of the North Wales & Liverpool Railway to Bidston, also backed by the MS&LR/GCR.

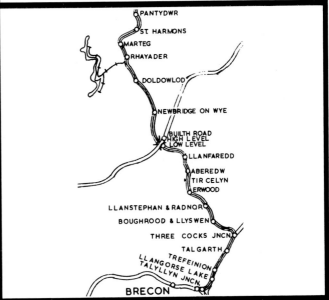

The author believes most firmly that no other form of graphic art is more evocative, or more informative, than a map.

These maps are alas only compromises between the problems of jamming in as much information as possible and of legibility for those of us whose eyesight is no longer what it was.

They cover a time-span of more than 200 years and not all of the enterprises depicted were working at the same time; nor did the track layouts shown mostly in simplified forms remain necessarily unaltered throughout their working lives. Mines and works could have their names changed more than once. Many have been omitted because rail connection seemed unlikely or could not as yet be substantiated.

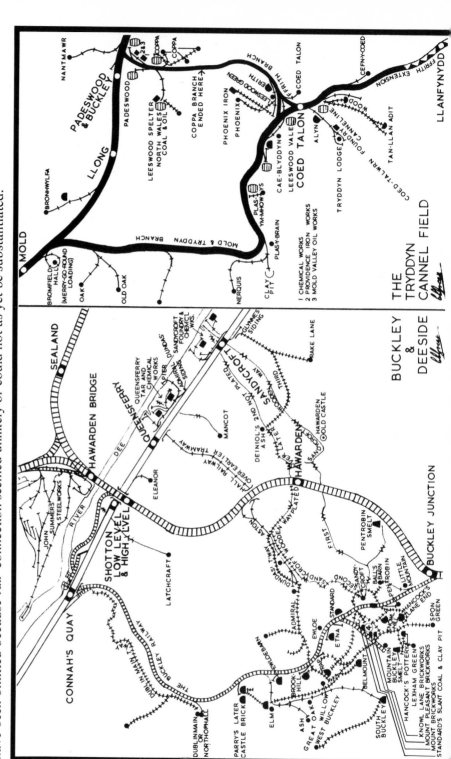

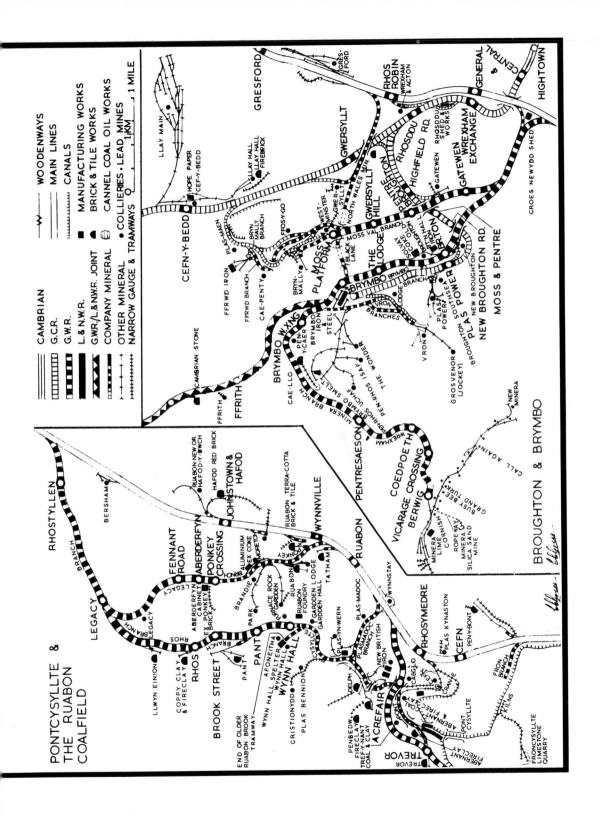

PONTCYSYLLTE &
THE RUABON
COALFIELD

The Forerunners -
The Early Tramways

Tramway is the accepted modern expression derived from old dialect usage of tram as a beam. Whether it came from old Norse tramn (Cleasby and Vigfusson) or from the Scottish tram which seemed to have been any small structural crosspiece in carpentry we may never know. North in 1742 writes of 'laying rails straight and parallel' and of 'Bulky Carts made with four Rowlets fitting these rails'. Dr Johnson's dictionary came after the devising of such things but to him in 1755 a rail was a part of a fence, a bird, and a woman's upper garment.

The similarity of beams laid parallel along the ground to the rails of a fence laid flat is obvious and Taylor in 1852 refers to earlier writers terming them as 'rail-ways'.

In the area we are going to look at tramway was not the accepted expression and the term was probably imposed upon the entire country by the ordnance surveyors. No one researcher is ever going to be the ultimate authority for so little has been documented except by chance and always a fresh proposition will arise to be examined, and to modify what the author has written.

Top right: The Mancot Woodenway (c1700-c1750) conveyed coal to the Dee and small sailboats took it to Chester upriver. The route has survived as roadways and the Chester & Holyhead had to bridge it so plating may have extended its life up to c1840. The boys are going to fetch turf from the river bank.

Centre right: The Latchcraft Woodenway is still visible as a stain of coal dust across the fields. Operative c1700-c1770.

Bottom right: The first Sandycroft Woodenway (c1750-c1780) climbed into a defence fosse below Hawarden Old Castle and probably was the only tramway to re-use part of an antiquity. Later came a counter re-usage for the Victorian park wall straddled the Broughton Brook over one of the abandoned tramway bridges.

Top left: The second Sandycroft Woodenway (c1780-c1845) took an improved route and was plated c1802 to 3ft 6in gauge which became the standard for the area. Called a rail-road on a map of 1816 it climbed out of Groomsdale along this ledge above Kearsley Farm before burrowing under the Ewloe Road through c100yd of brick-lined tunnel.

Top right: It has left this fine embankment at Deinol's Ash as evidence of its passing.

Above left: The third Sandycroft Rail Road (c1845-c1880) diverted the second at a colliery at Deiniol's Ash to a parallel route leading to Glynne's Siding. Sandycroft was silting up and the carriage of coal, bricks and tiles had been filtered off over Admiral Dundas' line. Taken near the vanished farmstead called **Scotland**.

Above right: Admiral Dundas' Rail Road (c1790-c1890) went to his better shipping facilities at Queensferry. An agreement of 1809 evidences an additional 'Railway or Road of cast iron' being laid 'to join the present Rail Road of Charles Dundas'. Later documents treat of 'The Buckley and Aston Railway', 'The Buckley and Aston Railroad', 'The Aston Tramway Company' and the words Tramroad and Tramway were also used.

Below left: Later the lower section became steam worked but above Aston Hall Colliery the cast iron was replaced by 12ft long wrought L section plateway. Lengths may still be found as stiles, fences, or even as bean poles.

Below right: The Dublin Main Tramway (c1830-c1862) was partly overlaid by The Buckley Railway and so became the only one to have any effect on the future shape of the railways of the district. Farmers waste nothing and the deep cutting provides a cost-free tip.
All C. C. Green

The Cambrian Railways Branches

The company was formed in 1864 by the amalgamation of five little systems and collected others later as already related in *Cambrian Railways Album*. Its branches were diverse and delightful in appearance and were equally diverse in their reasons for being.

Right: Aberdovey Sands Siding or Harbour Branch (1867-1964) was where you could paddle, build sandcastles and be photographed in front of a huge express engine. Afterwards you could watch ships being unloaded and watch the shunting — if you were very careful. *Anon*

Below right: The Dolgelley Branch (1868-1965) bore long trains from and to the cities of the north besides the little locals to Barmouth. A 'Small Sharp Stewart' conveying a train of mixed stock as far as Dolgelley where a Great Western engine will take over. Arthog c1905. *Courtesy of Ifor Higgon*

Bottom right: The Elan Valley Branch (1894-1917) was built specially for the Birmingham Corporation Water Works. Cambrian engines took the loaded trucks to Neuadd Sidings and brought back empties. *Courtesy of R. E. Thomas*

Left: Beyond Neuadd Sidings Birmingham engines took trains on to strange destinations along strange routes. The massive blocks of stone which shower spray off the outer face of Caban Coch Dam were railway bearers. *Nantgwyllt*, Hunslet 0-6-0T No 618 of 1894. *Anon*

Below: The Kerry Branch (1863-1956) was very much a local country branch and its principal business lay in the sheep of the upper valley. GW 0-6-0ST No 2075 heads Cambrian 'Small Sharp Stewart' No 21 as GW No 1118 with empty cattle vans past Fronfaith on 13 September 1929. *Ifor Higgon*

Bottom: Take a short trailing spur on a gradient, a wooden stage, a weighing machine and a wheelbarrow; and a country coal merchant has all he needs. GW 0-6-0 'Dean Goods' No 2556 shunting at Goitre on the Kerry. Fittingly the nearest wagon reminds us of 'Davies The Ocean' who built much of the Cambrian. *W. A. Camwell*

The Llanfyllin Branch (1863-1965)

Sheep and goods made in the wool mills were the mainstays of traffic but the mills closed before very long. Materials for the Vyrnwy Reservoir gave figures a boost for a short time and there was a notable brewery which gave rise to the temperance jibe 'old ale fills Llanfyllin with new widows'. Specially timed trains conveyed children to and from Llanfyllin's famous grammar school

Above: The arrival of the 8.23am ex-Llanymynech school train at Llansaintffraid on 27 July 1963.
C. C. Green

Right: When the branch was being rebuilt to give a direct approach from Llanymynech Irish navvies had shocked the townsfolk deeply by carousing in their lineside cabin. A young girl dressed in white and carrying a lighted candle knocked on the door. It was opened and she read a passage from the Holy Book, doused the candle, flung a black cloak about her and fled into the night as if all the fiends in hell were after her. And so they might have been had they known who had confronted them and had they not been too terror-struck by the apparition. Thereafter the good folk of Llanymynech were given back their peaceful Sunday evenings and many others were afeared to walk near the line by night. The junction just before closure. *C. C. Green*

Bottom right: GW Collett 0-4-2T No 5816 of 1933 about to leave Llanymynech with a Llanfyllin train on 3 October 1937. An empty Gresford wagon from Clwyd stands in the Shropshire & Montgomeryshire terminus. *Courtesy of R. S. Carpenter*

16

The Mawddwy Branch (1867-1950)

The privately-owned Mawwddwy Railway dealt with sheep and local goods but always the slate off the Hendre-ddu Tramway (page 90) was its mainstay. There were school trains to Cemmes Road with the extra fun of changing on to the Cambrian to go on down to Machynlleth. The Cambrian absorbed it in 1911 and the school trains then ran through to Machynlleth.

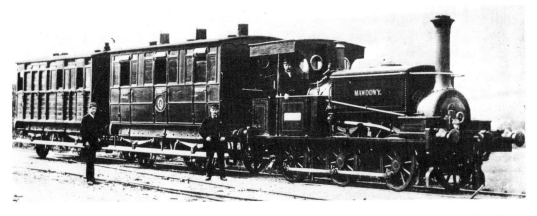

Above: Train at Cemmes Road around 1901. Manning Wardle 0-6-0ST No 140 of 1864.
Courtesy of L. T. George

Below: Cambrian 2-4-0 'Sharp Stewart' No 28 at Dinas Mawddwy c1912 with two Cambrian coaches and the guard-cum-parcels van. *G. M. Perkins*

The Mid Wales Branch (1864-1967)

The Mid Wales Railway was a rival to the Manchester and Milford's dream of north to south connection (page 80). Its only local commerce came from flour mills, timber and chemicals. It stayed in being as a useful but scarcely remunerative connecting line but a truly delightful journey for all its life.

Left: A 'Large Sharp Stewart' 4-4-0 with a train of six-wheeled coaches for Moat Lane passing Llanelwedd around 1895. *Courtesy of R. E. Thomas*

Below: Goods trains were never over-long except in wartime. 0-6-0 'Dean Goods' No 2483 of 1896 about to enter Marteg tunnel on the 9am Talyllyn Junction to Moat Lane goods 26 April 1952. *Ifor Higgon*

Bottom: Weakness in the bridges restricted motive power to the lighter engines. Cambrian 'Jones Goods' No 102 as GW No 896 entering Newbridge-on-Wye with the 2.40pm Moat Lane to Brecon 15 September 1949. *W. A. Camwell*

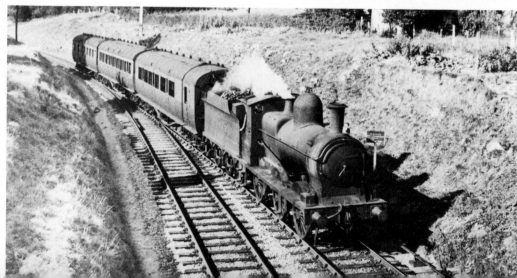

Above: Activity at Builth Road. GW 0-6-0 'Dean Goods' No 2556 has the 1.10pm Brecon to Moat Lane while LMR Stanier Class 5 4-6-0 No 45298 waits above with the 12.30pm Shrewsbury to Swansea alongside the train from Swansea on 15 September 1949.
W. A. Camwell

Below: When the Cambrian went into London Midland Region in 1962 many duties formerly worked by the lighter Great Western engines fell to the efficient little Ivatt Class 2 2-6-0s. No 46507 crossing 'A' bridge, Afon Dulas on the 1.20pm Brecon to Moat Lane 14 July 1962. *C. C. Green*

Top: The Nantmawr Branch (1866-   ) was part of the Shrewsbury, Potteries & North Wales Railway and its importance as a quarry outlet caused its absorption by the Cambrian. 0-6-0 'Sharp Stewart' No 14 *Broneirion* as GW No 898 by the wooden water tower which survived until the lighter pannier tanks took over. Seen on 7 May 1935. Later a diesel shunter grumbled its way up through the woods 'as required'; now the mineral trains load at Blodwell Quarry and are usually hauled by Class 25's. *V. R. Webster*

Above: The Porthywaen Branch (1863-1964) was a very short branch with a very big traffic in limestone and a very complicated junction. Left — The Tanat Valley and Nantmawr. Right of box — Machine Sidings and works and stores. Just past the box — Branch through embankment climbing up into Pear Tree Quarry. Climbing away out of sight — Original Porthywaen Branch to Cooper Quarry with several trailing spurs. Straight on at lower level — Remains of three track loop sidings (some derelict wagons). Near curving right — Later track into Pear Tree Quarry. Originally the 2ft 6in Crickheath Tramway was a little to the left of the Tanat line and crossed over to follow the course of the line through the embankment. *Ivor Higgon*

Above: The Scafell Branch (c1863-1937) trailed from the down side to Penstrowed Quarry and had to be worked by down goods only. (See also *Cambrian Railways Album Vol 2* page 92.) *C. C. Green*

Below: The Sweeney Branch (1861-c1885) can be detected only by the eye of faith as a low trace curving away from the second telegraph pole south of Weston Wharf. It served brickworks and a colliery. *C. C. Green*

The Tanat Valley Branch (1904-1951)

Built under the Light Railways Act with flat-bottomed rail it was very much a countryside affair. How the country folk could use railways to have a day's outing comes out clearly in this brief account. 'As children we would walk the two miles to Porthywaen and take the train to Llangynog whence we set out on the 14 miles over the Berwyns to Bala Junction. Another train took us to Ruabon and we travelled then down to Gobowen and so at last to Oswestry. The final walk home was around three miles'. Besides the charm of its scenery it retained the last two Cambrian tank engines which just, and only just, survived to be scrapped by British Railways.

Far left, top: 2-4-0 'Sharp Stewart' tank No 59 *Seaham* as GW No 1197 built in 1866 with a train of GW four-wheelers on Porthywaen crossing in 1947. *Selwyn Higgins*

Far left, bottom: The same engine takes a neat little goods train away from Llangynog in 1935. The leading wagon is Burton & Co. *W. A. Camwell*

Above: The Trefonen Branch (1863-1869) was built as a private railway by the contractor Thomas Savin to serve his New British Coal Pit in the Morda Valley. This and the Sweeney Colliery (page 21) were the only collieries left to the Cambrian and they were soon worked out. *R. E. Thomas*

Left: The Tonfanau Quarry Branch (c1898-1964) was a 2ft gauge line with a vertical boilered engine *Freda* until 1906. Here an 0-6-0 'Aston Goods' propels 18 empty wagons up to the quarry around 1925. The sidings were usable but scarcely used up to the closure date given but the date of the last train up to the quarry has not so far been traced. *Courtesy of H. B. Evans*

23

The Wrexham Branch (1895-1962)

The Wrexham & Ellesmere Railway took 10 years from authorisation to opening. Operated by the Cambrian it was intended as one of the north to south links in Edward Watkin's Welsh Railway Union. The six Nasmyth Wilson 0-4-4 tanks built for the line nearly came out as 4-4-0 tanks. A 'goods only' service ran after 1962 from Wrexham to Cadbury's.

Above: 'Wrexham Tankie' No 7 in Caia Goods c1900. Note the stoutly-built tannery wagon with the arched front lettered J. Meredith-Jones & Sons.
Courtesy of J. Meredith-Jones

Below: The high viaducts were landmarks as one approached Wrexham. Even then the Cambrian still instigated designs for double track. A GW 0-4-2T propels the 4.20pm ex-Ellesmere across the Clywedog on 8 September 1962, the last day of the service.
C. C. Green

Top: More sadly, the last train. Under an evening sky GW 0-4-2T No 4832 as WR No 1432 propels the 7.25pm ex-Ellesmere out of Marchwiel to a civic ceremony in Wrexham and a return to Ellesmere with four well-filled coaches. *C. C. Green*

Above: Being of late construction the work came into the period of the amateur photographer and a Mr Berry recorded several scenes. *Dorothy*, an 0-4-0 Hunslet saddle tank at 'end of track'. Even the Clywedog and Kings Mill Viaducts were first built as temporary light-weight trestle bridges. *Clwyd Record Office*

The Van Branch (1871-1940)

The Van was one of the great lead mines of Wales requiring a large complex of mills and machinery. It just lasted into the railway era and the Van Railway opened with an as yet unknown engine. The price of lead slumped and the line closed in 1893 to be re-opened by the Cambrian in 1896.

Above: The mineworks c1885. In the centre we look down the launder which conveyed water from the Tarannon to the great wheel. This cranked a slide-rest which pushed and pulled the long drive rod up and down on its bearing pulleys working the deep water pump which drained the mine shaft behind the camera. As the rod was forced uphill balance weights fell to give a near-perfect kinetic balance. *Powys County Library*

Below: Manning Wardle 0-6-0ST No 668 of 1877 at Caersws. When the Cambrian took her over as their No 25 they transferred the ornate doric fluted safety-valve cover from the earlier engine so giving rise to the legend that it had been No 374 of 1871 that had survived. *Courtesy of Ifor Higgon*

The Great Central Branches

The Buckley Railway (1862-1965)

The brickworks and colliery owners of Buckley were in the grip of a monopoly engineered by Dundas (page 13) who had lured them away from the second (Glynne) Sandycroft Tramway with the much better quay facilities he could offer at Queensferry. The Dublin Main Colliery had already solved its problem by making a steep tramway down to Golftyn where an Irishman, one Connah or Cunnah had a small quay. Encouraged by Sir Stephen Glynne they formed their own company to build a railway to Connah's Quay. Also they formed the Buckley Traders Association to own special wagons for mutual use and to regulate their dealings with the railway. Powers were taken to carry passengers but these were rarely invoked for special occasions. Gradients were excessive and curves over-sharp. In 1873 the line was leased to the Wrexham, Mold & Connah's Quay Railway for 999 years.

Above left: A 'shipping wagon' belonging to The Buckley Traders' Association. The open-sided 'shipping boxes' on grooved wheels were kept in place by battens at the track ends but principally by the drop-bars pivotted in the ends. *Martin Mollington*

Left: The Ewloebarn Company's Brickworks (all were known locally as 'brikils') showing the step in the loading quay and the traverser wagon which carried a pair of rails matching those down the brikil yards and on the shipping wagons. *Courtesy of James Bentley*

27

Above: At Connah's Quay in 1876, 'The Buckley Railway Company's Dock for shipping bricks'. WM&CQR open wagons on the left and shipping wagons on the right. *Martin Mollington*

Below: Connah's Quay in the 1890s. Wharfingers are fending away the loaded schooner which the tug will tow downstream casting off near Point of Air for Ireland or Liverpool etc. Idle for the moment are the quadruple-sling cranes which lift the shipping boxes by the corner-eyes and lower them into the schooners. A few empty shipping boxes stand out of the way on the right on extra 'pushaway' narrow gauge tracks. Loaded shipping wagons await the next ship alongside. Two men from the brikil went to the destination port with each cargo to eliminate careless handling of pipes, tiles and other fragile clayware. *Clwyd Record Office*

Above: Dublin Main Siding in 1876. As evidence in a dispute with the WM&CQR the Association had commissioned a Chester photographer to make a pictorial survey. *Martin Mollington*

Below: The Mount Pleasant Colliery extension built by the WM&CQR. No 6 with wagons named for the owner instead of for his colliery in the 1890s.
Courtesy of James Bentley

Above: For their locomotives the Buckley went to the newly reorganised firm of Hudswell, Clarke & Co Ltd for Works Nos 2 and 3 of 1861 named *Wheatley* and *Kenyon*. No 1 as WM&CQR No 1 at Ffrith. *Courtesy of R. E. Thomas*

Below: Great Eastern Holden Class R24 0-6-0T No 258 of 1899 as LNER Class J67 No 68585 on a small goods at Buckley Old Station on 4 May 1957. *G. H. Platt*

The Wrexham, Mold & Connah's Quay Railway (1862-   )

The overnight success of the Buckley Railway created new demands for rail connection with Connah's Quay from brickworks, ironworks and collieries nearer Wrexham. Starting with the Wrexham, Mold & Connah's Quay Junction Railway opened in 1862 there became by 1900 a very useful straggly system which connected with nearly every major company in the area. Also to the delight of monopoly-bound concerns it wriggled its way round, over and under the established Great Western preserves to the north-west of Wrexham.

Alas! another company's supporters were on the board and the other directors were not astute enough to have the system properly maintained or to see where they were being led. In 1889 they were lured into a joint undertaking for a line from Bidston later called the North Wales and Liverpool. The Manchester, Sheffield & Lincolnshire did build it and charged interest on the capital, put their stock on to work it and charged for that too. In 1897 they put the Receiver in and in 1905 the Great Central took over. Edward Watkin had triumphed again (page 6).

Above: The train that foreshadowed the end of the WM&CQR Company. The special train waiting in Hawarden station to take Mr and Mrs Gladstone to the formal opening ceremonies of the North Wales and Liverpool on 28 March 1896. 2-4-0 No 89 Class 1B rebuilt from a South Yorkshire engine.
From Great Central Vol II by George Dow

Right: A few of the old engines off the WM&CQ survived into the grouping period but generally the line assumed the Robinson look. Class C13 4-4-2T No 1056 as LNER Class 9K No 6056 on a train to Wrexham at Buckley Junction c1935. *R. E. Thomas*

Top: At Hope Exchange passengers descended a
footpath to the L&NWR station below called Hope
Exchange Low Level. GC Robinson Class C13
4-4-2T No 359 of 1905 as LNER Class 9K No 7436 on
a train for Wrexham. *W. A. Camwell*

Above: Hope Village was $2\frac{1}{4}$ miles further south.
Another of the same, No 357 as No 7435 with the
1.28pm Seacombe to Wrexham, 13 March 1948. These
Class 9Ks were nice steady free-running engines, liked by
their crews and capable of holding some tight schedules.
W. A. Camwell

Above: Wrexham (Exchange), the original **WM&CQ** terminus with No 455 of 1905 as BR No E7432 on the 2.30pm Seacombe to Wrexham Central 7 August 1948. *W. A. Camwell*

Below: Wrexham Central also was the southern goods terminus; the extension from Wrexham (Exchange) was opened in 1888. GC Parker Class 9F 0-6-2T No 938 of 1900 as LNE Class N5 No 9362 seen 13 March 1948. A crew whose engine had failed was sent out with a partly-depleted replacement. 'You will be all right' the foreman said, 'it is a coal train you are bringing in from Llay'. It was, — full of best house nuts. 'Try as we would, we could not keep that fire down on the bars. Every time my driver tried to open her up it danced and the nuts flew up the tubes. They rattled off the bridges, they bounced off the station roofs. I reckon we filled every gutter from Llay to Wrexham'. These too were good solid steady engines. *W. A. Camwell*

Top: Passengers on the L&NW main line could look down upon the Connah's Quay Branch. GC Robinson Class 5A 0-6-0T No 538 of 1906 as BR No 68209 in January 1954. *H. F. Wheeller*

Above left: A last look — the old WM&CQ Brymbo Branch terminus around 1900 is still a little oasis between the great steel works and the Great Western line. *The Geoffrey Charles Collection, The National Library of Wales*

Above right: By comparison — the ever advancing slag heaps had engulfed it all by 1935. *R. E. Thomas*

Below: At first the WM&CQ also went to Hudswell Clarke's for its engines and collected some very attractive individuals. No 4 started as an 0-6-0T HC No 16 of 1863 named *Lord Richard*; temporarily lost a bit off the back and the trailing wheels after an accident in 1884 and was restored to balance as an 0-4-2T in 1889. *Courtesy of R. E. Thomas*

Top left: The Chester & Holyhead bridged the Dublin Main Tramway with adequate headroom for horses but even possible subsequent works did not give enough headroom for a full height steam locomotive. No 7 *Duke* without a cab could get on to Connah's Quay. Hudswell Clarke No 189 of 1878. *Courtesy of R. E. Thomas*

Centre left: No 9 *Dee* HC 119 of 1872 bought second-hand from Thos Butlin & Co was also low enough to get through and is seen here actually on Connah's Quay. *Courtesy of R. E. Thomas*

Below: Of the heavier engines No 8 *Premier* was Sharp Stewart 0-6-0T No 2932 of 1880, seen here as GC No 405C. The second engine was another changeling. No 6 *Queen* was built as a Sharp Roberts 0-6-0ST in 1846, for the Manchester and Birmingham and the WM&CQ bought her as L&NW No 1829 in 1872. They rebuilt her as an 0-8-0ST in 1880 and as an 0-6-2ST in 1888. In 1903 she was restored to an 0-8-0ST as seen here as GC No 400B. *W. H. Whitworth*

The Great Western Branches

The WM&CQ account has given us an introduction to the practices of 'the heavy brigade' and now we shall be very much concerned with the interplay between grasping remote managements uncaring about local matters except to make a profit out of them. Thwarted by the Gauge Commission (page 6) Paddington still wanted (1) a route westwards across North Wales (2) the mineral trade of Clwyd (Denbighshire and Flintshire) and (3) the Festiniog slate traffic.

It achieved the first ambition to the partial detriment of the Cambrian's main line and a fair bit of local goods traffic was ensnared from the L&NW's longer connection via Afon Wen; but traffic over the Ruabon Branch never attained main line status. It did very well in Clwyd by getting there first. Pursuit of ambition No 3 landed it with a fascinating little line but not much profit.

Neither Paddington nor Euston could understand that the Festiniog Railway had been promoted by and was run for the quarry companies who were also its principal shareholders. For them the titles Great Western and London & North Western held no magic.

The Bala Branch (1883-1965)

The Great Western referred to many of its branches by where they started from rather than where they went. Promoted as the Bala & Festiniog Railway this branch was built end on to the narrow gauge Festiniog & Blaenau and the latter was ripped up and re-formed in standard gauge. The unsuitability of the site at Manod forced the GW to build transporter trucks to take the 1ft $11\frac{1}{2}$in gauge slate wagons to Festiniog, at best for transhipment, but often only for transmission on to the Festiniog.

Trawsfynydd is still connected to Blaenau Ffestiniog for a special goods service. (Page 40.)

Left: The Festiniog & Blaenau train at Tan-y-manod; possibly the opening day 30 May 1868, there are around 200 people standing by or perched precariously on a score of attached slate wagons.
C. Thomas. The National Library of Wales

Above: No 973, a 2-4-0 'Metropolitan' tank of 1874, running around a train of six-wheelers at Blaenau Festiniog c1929. *J. R. Hollick*

two separate trains are being worked as one. *J. I. C. Boyd*

Below: A surprisingly long mixed train at Arenig in May 1950. The leading engine is GW No 7416 of 1936, and

Bottom: And the shortest of mixed trains near Llan Festiniog 20 September 1948. *C. F. H. Oldham*

Above: A goods for Blaenau Ffestiniog (as it should always have been spelt) coasts off the great Cwm Prysor viaduct; a typical grey mountain day when the lightest thing to be seen is the exhaust steam from GW No 5774, of the heavier '57XX' class of 1929. April 1959.
J. I. C. Boyd

Right: Two to be picked up at Teigl Halt in 1959; hardly worth the wear on the brake shoes. Note the fogman's hut, the line could be in cloud for days on end and crossing Cwm Prysor one felt as if the carriage was the gondola of an airship suspended over a grey void.
G. H. Platt

Below: This was of course just the sort of weather to attract the army and there was an artillery training camp with its own platform at Trawsfynydd.
Courtesy of M. E. M. Lloyd

Above: Approaching Manod; the conical tump on the right was the sign that soon the long winding journey would be over. Note the continuous check-rail. WR No 7440 was the first of the last batch of these engines built in 1950. *R. C. Riley*

Below: Bala Junction could offer the sight of quite a bit of carriage shunting as the train strength in any direction was adjusted to suit requirements. GW No 4683 of 1944 propelling a brake composite ex-Bala on 28 July 1951. *R. C. Riley*

Top: Motive power was not quite confined to the various versions of the pannier tank. GW 0-6-0 'Collett Goods' No 3207 of 1946 at Blaenau Festiniog with full pressure up to take the 7.15pm to Bala 7 August 1948. *W. A. Camwell*

Above: The needs of atomic power has occasioned at long last the joining of the GW to the L&NW in Blaenau Ffestiniog and the preservation of the far fag-end of the line. No D5001, BR Class 24 of 1958 propels an empty atomic waste container up to Trawsfynydd 28 Ocotber 1968. *N. F. Gurley*

Right: A survival from the once-prosperous woollen mills. *Courtesy of E. W. Hannan*

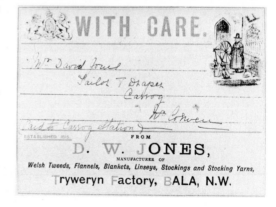

WITH CARE.

Mr David Jones
Tailor & Draper
Carrog
Nr Corwen

Send to Carrog Station

ESTABLISHED 1815.

FROM

D. W. JONES,

MANUFACTURER OF

Welsh Tweeds, Flannels, Blankets, Linseys, Stockings and Stocking Yarns,

Tryweryn Factory, BALA, N.W.

40

Brymbo and the Wrexham Area

The Great Western bought its way in most successfully and consolidated its position by improvement and extension. The map on page 9 shows the result more clearly than a long verbose explanation bestrewn with indecodable abbreviations.

Above: Initially the North Wales Mineral had two slight inclines and trucks were rope-hauled through two tunnels. Two years after opening a small engine named *Charlotte* was working right through. She could have been either of two Shrewsbury & Chester small engines. In 1852 she was hit by a runaway wagon and two of the three men on her footplate were killed. The Great Western eliminated this risk working by building the Wrexham & Minera Branch. At first the abandoned tunnels were left open and it was recorded by Mr Ifor Edwards, headmaster of the Brymbo and Broughton British School 'that a number of boys and girls had met in the evenings in the tunnel and had ginger beer etc with them. There was also some screaming and noise and it was probable that their object in collecting in that dark place was anything but a good one'. He soon put a stop to that and checked by going into the tunnel himself. The

Brymbo end of Summerhill (Brake) tunnel 11 July 1959. *R. W. Miller*

Below: To avoid priming through the safety valves on the steep line the fireman would have let the water level down as low as was safe, the driver would take her up at a good clip and the injector would be put hard on as soon as the top level had been attained.

One severe winter the train had stuck, snow plough and all in a deep drift. The works manager badly needed the raw materials and waved a ten-shilling note (50p) in front of the driver to overcome his reluctance to risk a derailment. After three good bashes the train went through. The fireman got only half a crown (12½p). 'After all', claimed the driver, 'it was my responsibility'. Brymbo Steelworks Sidings in 1957. *G. H. Platt*

Above: Berwig Halt, the last one on the Wrexham & Minera Branch was a real tiny country outpost. Served by rail motor it closed at the end of 1930.
Pearces Series

Left: Barely a quarter of a mile past Berwig was the end at Minera Lima Works whence a spur once reversed to the Minera Lead Mines. The name Minera is said to have arisen from a mis-reading of an early map which showed 'Mine Area'. No 4683 waiting to draw into the limeworks yard in 1963. *J. I. C. Boyd*

Below: Local deposits of iron ore and coal ran out years ago but Brymbo Steel Works kept going on 'imports'. BR No 24.063, a Class 24 of 1958 leaving with empties for Croes Newydd 12 July 1976. The line is still open for goods only. *Tom Heavyside*

Top left: Competitive duplication at Plas Power; the linking crossover between the GW (left) and the GC ex-WM&CQ (right). *R. W. Miller*

Centre left: Croes Newydd was the home of several little 0-4-0ST's kept going as long as possible for the minor colliery branches and sidings. The fireman's side (whichever that was) was sheeted in so that more coal could be stacked on the footplate. No 96 was once Birkenhead Railway No 39 *Cricket*, Sharp Stewart No 964 of 1856. In for regulator repairs in 1914. *P. W. Robinson*

Below: Later colliery work was done by standard 0-6-0 pannier tanks which have been much lauded as marvels of small-scale efficiency; but — 'You bang your backside and crack your right elbow on the bunker front, scrape your left leg on the sandbox and catch your left knee on the springs. For good luck as you put the injector on the worn valve wheels tear your fingers'. Former Class 655 saddle tank No 1780 of 1893, c1925. *J. P. Richards*

Above: The Pontcysyllte Branch served the Monsanto Chemical Works which was another nightmare for the crews. The train went up before breakfast because anything eaten at Croes Newydd before setting out was lost over the side when they got into the stench. At the Trefrnant Viaduct the driver had to stop way back if it was teeming with rain and the wind was funnelling down the cwm and blowing the sand off the rails. The unfortunate fireman had to walk down the dip and up along the climbing viaduct to throw the points for the yard; no way could a starting grip be got below the points. After a suitable wait the driver opened up and tore down the dip and up the viaduct and if he didn't get there before his fireman all was well. If not !!!**? The horse tramway bridge (1805-1860) was much lower and the line curved round to the right and terminated at a crane which hoisted the waggon up to a higher reversing track while the horse walked up a ramp. The branch closed in 1968. *C. C. Green*

Below: From 1848 until 1965 the Gobowen Branch had a tiny shuttle service partly from Ruabon to Oswestry and mostly with 'All Change' at both ends. It linked Oswestry with the GW main services and bore a fair goods traffic in coal from the Wrexham area to anywhere on the north eastern end of the Cambrian and down the Mid Wales. It remains intact to connect with a disjointed track with chopped off bits of points which weaves uncertainly through Oswestry for the occasional Nantmawr/Blodwell goods. Collett 0-4-2T No 1458, formerly No 4858 of 1935 in the Oswestry bay with a single coach 'train' in 1964. *R. Storer*

The Ruabon Branch (1868-1968)

Once the baseline, Shrewsbury-Wrexham-Chester, had been won it was a comparatively simple matter for the Great Western to mastermind lines aiming west and to take them over. Construction of the Llangollen & Corwen, of the Corwen & Bala and the Bala & Dolgelley was relatively easy and end-to-end junction with the Cambrian at Dolgelley gave a reasonable though slow to work single line to the north end of Cardigan Bay, but it could never equal the London & North Western's coastal race track to Holyhead.

Latterly the enginemen called it 'The Barmouth Road'.

Above: A splendid signboard awaited passengers at the south end of Ruabon station. An auto train from Oswestry, one of the Wrexham or Chester through services, entering 23 July 1951. *R. C. Riley*

Left: The track was double to Llangollen. Here we can enjoy the sight of a backlit plume of steam as a 4-4-0 'Bulldog' gets smartly under way towards Ruabon, seen c1930. *J. P. Richards*

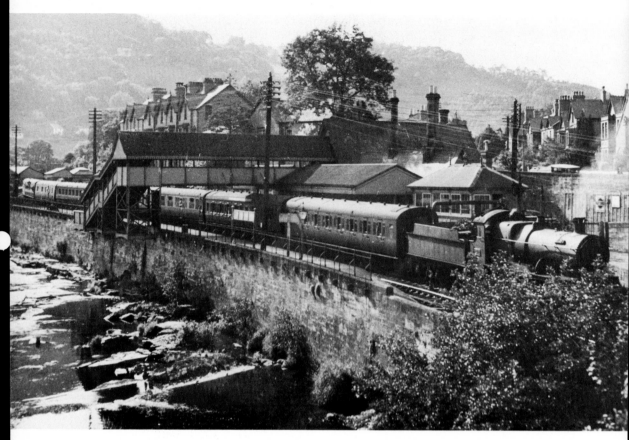

Above: Considering the importance of Llangollen as a
wool town it did not get a very large station. 2-6-0 Mogul
No 5322 of 1917 on the 2.35pm from Barmouth,
7 August 1948. *W. A. Camwell*

Below: Corwen too was an important town and here we
see the famous scissor crossing which sorted the trains
from Chester, Denbigh and Rhyl curving in from the left
and running single-track alongside the GW line before
arriving over the crossing. LMS Class 2P No 675 of
1932 brings in the 5.12pm ex Denbigh on 7 August
1948. *W. A. Camwell*

Above: In 1889 Her Majesty Queen Victoria made a formal visit to Central Wales and Llandderfel had its moments of glory for Pale House where she was staying was but half a mile away. Both the GW and the L&NW Royal trains were used working from Corwen. Prince Henry and Princess Beatrice of Battenburg and Princess Alice of Hesse also visited the only Denbighshire colliery to have a Royal visit, the Wynnstay. 0-6-0PT No 7409 of 1936 brings in a more prosaic train, a stopping goods from Ruabon. *Dr Ian C. Allen*

Below: In more recent times Llandderfel was the scene of a great tragedy. The signalman rushed up to the crew of **a Barmouth-bound Mogul clutching the promised brace** of pheasants. 'Here! Take these' he exclaimed with a backward jerk of his head. A quick glance down the platform revealed the police sergeant proceeding towards the engine. 'Good morning sergeant'. 'Good morning, may I have a look around your cab please?' 'Of course sergeant, come up'. 'And may I have a look in your toolboxes?' 'Do by all means'. He opened the boxes and looked carefully under the contents. He moved a few pieces of coal. He looked down from the other side and by now the crew were looking at their watches. He gave up and got down on to the platform.

As the train drew away a few charred feathers fluttered out of the smoke on to the lineside. What else could they have done? Llandderfel station on Boxing Day 1964. *W. A. Camwell*

Top: Once past Bala Lake the line climbed to its summit at Garneddwen. Mogul No 5319 leaving Garneddwen for Barmouth Junction, 11 September 1937. *Ifor Higgon*

Above: Thence it was downhill all the way to the coast. No 5315, yet another of Lot 206, lifting the 2.35pm ex-Dolgelley out of Drws-y-nant 31 January 1957. During World War 1 there was here a brisk traffic in timber. *W. A. Camwell*

Below: Bontnewydd was enlarged and a passing loop put in as part of the 1920s plan to provide a heavier Blue route to Cardigan Bay (*Cambrian Railways Album Vol 2*). 4-6-0 No 7817 *Garsington Manor*, exactly six months old on one of the very early 'Manor' workings 1 July 1939. To while away long waits in the loops some crew members would pick flowers and bedeck the smoke box to give the engine a holiday look. *Ifor Higgon*

Above: At Dolgelley (now Dolgellau) the Barmouth local could be seen. Collett 0-4-2T No 1434 about to start the 8.30am 9 August 1948. *W. A. Camwell*

Below: After 1922 the entire route had been operated as the Ruabon Branch. A 2-6-0 'Aberdare' of c1902 bringing a goods from Ruabon into Barmouth Junction c1928. *J. P. Richards*

The London & North Western Branches from the Coast

Once the Chester & Holyhead had been gathered in expansion into the mineral producing areas began.

Afon Wen and Nantlle (1867-1970)

Caernarfon joined the railway age with three separate systems which were joined up by the L&NW. The Bangor & Carnarvon of 1852 joined the Chester & Holyhead at Menai Bridge. The Carnarvonshire Railway started over half a mile away at Pant and had to end at Afon Wen instead of Portmadoc as first intended. 0-4-2 No 7 *Llanerchydol* and 2-4-0T No 59 *Seaham* had to be hired from the Cambrian to start the service. (See page 61 for the third line.) The attempt on Portmadoc may have failed but a lot of slate was carried from Nantlle and off the North Wales Narrow Gauge at Dinas Junction.

Left: The Crewe policy of building many small cheap engines meant that those designed later by Whale and Bowen-Cooke were principally larger main line types so releasing the little Francis Webb engines for a long life on the lesser lines. The Webb look at Tal-y-sarn in the 1890s. 0-6-2 'Coal Tank' No 2457 of 1886. *Gwynedd Archives Service*

Below left: Llanwrda was laid out on a narrow site and the two platforms were on opposite sides of the level crossing. *Courtesy of E. W. Hannan*

Top right: Some Standard class engines did get to Bangor near the end of steam much to the delight of the footplate men. Class 4 2-6-4T No 80090 of 1954 arriving at Chwilog on the 2.52pm ex-Bangor, 20 April 1957. *W. A. Camwell*

Centre right: The dwindling service ended as did so many with DMUs. A Derby Lightweight set leaving Afon Wen as the 20.35pm to Caernarfon. *C. C. Green*

Bottom right: Another scene at Tal-y-sarn in the 1890s provides a link with Clywd. The two wagons in the left foreground have brought coal from Broughton and Plas Power. *Gwynedd Archives Service and Courtesy of Mrs Eira Thomas*

Anglesey — The Amlwch Branch (1866-1964) & goods only 1964- and Red Wharf Bay (1908-1930)

George Stephenson had reported the line not worth building but the islanders wanted it. The Anglesey Central Railway started with only one locomotive but a very extraordinary one. *Anglesea* was the second 0-4-4-0 Fairlie to be built; an unhandy and temperamental machine which created the need for an L&NW takeover after only five years. By then the great Parys copper mine at Amlwch was failing and artificial fertiliser and chemicals were the only forms of heavy freight.

Its offshoot the Red Wharf Bay was a late little scheme foredoomed to failure. J. M. Dunn wrote in *The Railway Magazine* that 'passengers went there once by rail and thereafter returned by more convenient means of transport'. The terminus Red Wharf Bay and Benllech was at neither place. It just attained the age of majority and closed down; except for very small goods trains.

Top right: A Webb 2-4-2T about to leave Amlwch for Bangor. All trains crossed the Menai Bridge and after this racing Ramsbottom Singles and later the splendid 'Claughtons' could be seen so enlivening the otherwise peaceful journey across the ancient granary of the Princes of Gwynedd. September 1932. *G. H. Platt*

Centre right: 0-6-0 Webb No 3462 of 1878 as LMS No 8159 has shunted aside its insignificant goods train at Llangefni to allow through a passenger train to Almwch in April 1937. *G. H. Platt*

Below: Being given one of these engines in lieu of his clapped-out clanking bearing-hotting old Webb is stated to have converted the surliest of curmudgeons at Bangor shed into a normal happy individual. (J. M. Dunn.) LMS Ivatt 2-6-2T Class 2 No 1224 of 1948 as LMR No 41224 passing Holland Arms, March 1949. *J. I. C. Boyd*

Above: The Amlwch branch was the trial route for
DMUs in 1953 and the results were deemed highly
satisfactory. DMUs finally took over from steam in
1956. *J. I. C. Boyd*

Below: LNW 2-4-0T No 1000, rebuilt in 1908 from a
2-4-2T of 1884, motor-fitted and two special bogie cars
rebuilt from old Webb radial coaches leaving Holland

Arms at the start of the Red Wharf Bay service May
1913. *H. Thompson in The Railway Magazine*

Bottom: Soon only one coach was enough and a steam
rail motor ended the service. On bank holidays and some
market days the 'train' could get venturesome and
reverse north out of Holland Arms up to even as far as
Llangefni. Benllech terminus. *Real Photographs*

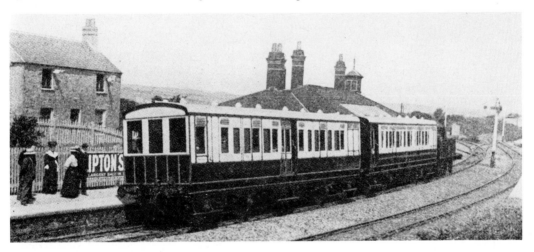

The Bethesda Branch (1884-1963)

This was another of Euston's wishful thinkings without an understanding of the local situation. Lord Penrhyn made stipulations including a maximum height for the junction signalbox, permissions to be got for the erection of telegraph poles and for many screening trees to avoid degrading His Lordship's scenery.

He was far too astute to fall for the idea that his Penrhyn Quarries should eschew the 1ft 11 in gauge (page 99) and that he should commit all his precious eggs to the L&NW's one monopolistic basket. Despite this it was at first called the Penrhyn branch.

Above: Webb 0-6-2 'Coal Tank' No 2463 of 1882 as LMR No 27602 about to propel its motor-fitted train back as the 8.10pm to Bangor 24 May 1957. *W. A. Camwell*

Below: Bethesda was one of the nicest of the little termini. The engine is believed to be ex-LMS Ivatt 2-6-2T No 41223. Seen on 10 May 1949. *E. S. Russell*

The Dyserth Branch (1869-1973)

It was first known as the Prestatyn & Cwm branch but earthworks only exist beyond the limestone quarry at Dyserth. A 'steam motor car' service ran from 1905 to 1930 for the highly-scenic run up the gorge and a visit to the castle which was once the stronghold of the Lords of Tegaingl. For its last few years it distinguished itself as the modellers' justification for running large locos on small layouts. The quarry was served by any loco that was to hand be it an ancient 0-6-0, a 'Jubilee' or a Class 8F 2-8-0; a glorious finale.

Left: The line was much publicised as a 'mountain railway'. Here the 'motor car' is running along the ledge on Craig Fawr. *Courtesy of F. E. Hemming*

Below: Beyond Dyserth traces of the proposed Newmarket extension remain still as evidence of country people's desire to be linked by rail to the rest of the community. Looking towards Pandy Mill 10 December 1977. *Trefor Thompson*

The Festiniog Branch (1879-   )

This unrewarding access to the slate of Festiniog was gained in three stages. The first was the Conway & Llanrwst to reach the zinc mines in 1863. The second extended to claim the rich tourist trade of (as then spelt) Bettws-y-coed. Then came the successful elimination of North Wales Narrow Gauge Railway No 1 by bulldozing through an outrageous scheme for an L&NW narrow gauge feeder. Perhaps Euston dreamt also of a middle-bit monopoly in a narrow gauge way from Portmadoc to Ruthin. In the event the scheme became one of the costliest pieces of construction in the country with a $2\frac{1}{4}$ mile long tunnel which ruined the first contractor. Despite the quarry owners' interest in the Festiniog Railway (page 36) 10ton wagons were fitted with transverse rails to carry three narrow-gauge slate wagons apiece northwards through that expensive tunnel. This fantasy was played out to the end with a special shipping quay bearing narrow-gauge tracks and turntables at Deganwy.

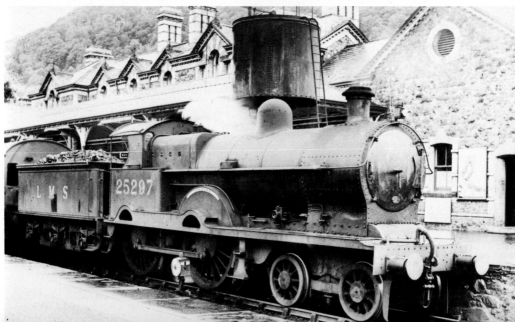

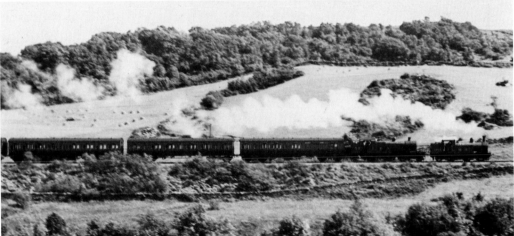

Top left: Dolgarrog was an insignificant little halt yet nearby was a branch to a great aluminium works with its own narrow gauge railway, an early tramway from lead mines and a railway which built a reservoir. Taken in 1964. *G. H. Platt*

Bottom left: Bettws-y-coed was THE station of the branch and even today still has its refreshment rooms. There must have been a loco shortage to cause the despatch of Whale 'Precursor' *Sirocco* No 643 of 1904 (here LMS No 25297) on 17 June 1947. It seems appropriate to relate a wartime story hitherto on the secret list. The Royal Engineers train men attached to the Royal Corps of Signals training camp near Rhyl were all on a Lewis gun training session. A little shunting had to be done in Rhyl Yard. A man who could do the job was detailed to volunteer. He was not told the engine would be a 'Precursor' with a steam shunting brake. They had a

nasty habit of snatching on at a crawl — and did. The luckless volunteer, powerless to avert *Sirocco's* gentle slide into the buffer stop, jammed hard up against the hot backplate and up to his shins in lumps of coal off the tender, was Lance-Corporal J. I. C. Boyd.
C. F. H. Oldham

Top: The down side of   Betws-y-coed (as it is now spelt) had been dismantled and now houses the Conwy Valley Museum. 0-6-2 Webb 'Coal Tank' No 3730 of 1897 as LMR No 7841 on 27 May 1951.
W. A. Camwell

Above: The beauty of the Lledr Valley was well-seen from the train. LMS Fowler Class 3P No 15551 of 1931 renumbered to 52 piloted by an 0-6-2 'Radial Tank' in 1938. *J. I. C. Boyd*

57

Above: After the tunnel through which early passengers were reassured by oil lamps hung outside the carriages came man-made desolation. Pant Fawr (with over 100 men standing on it) led to the slate mill to the right. Below this enormous tip the L&NW track is being raised some 8ft to be level with the top of the retaining wall by an ingenious method of tipping stone through the new track temporarily carried on timbers.
J. Thomas — The National Library of Wales

Below: The passenger station at Blaenau Ffestiniog was a large temporary wooden affair which lasted for nearly 100 years. LMS Stanier 2-6-2T Class 3P No 209 of 1938 as LMR No 40209 on the 7.55pm to Llandudno Junction 7 August 1948. *W. A. Camwell*

Below: Opposite lay the goods yard with narrow gauge tracks rising steeply on to the loading dock where there were originally the turntables for directing slate trucks on to standard gauge wagons. The nearer engine is 0-6-0 Webb No 2305 of 1895 as LMS No 8393. The next coach is a Midland clerestory. Seen on 23 July 1934. *C. F. H. Oldham*

Bottom: The yard shunter was mostly a Webb 0-6-0 18in goods or 'Cauliflower' or 'Crested Goods' a name said to have come from the over-herbaceous look of the crest — or was it a play on collier? No 553 of 1901 as LMR No 28589 on 23 July 1951. *R. C. Riley*

59

The Holywell Branch (1912-1954)

The L&NW revived powers of 1864 and used largely the route of an even older horse-worked line. It was very much a service for well-off commuters.

Above: Although engines could run round at the deadend in a little blank cut into the hillside passenger work was mostly done by auto trains. The rising trailing spur into the goods yard went off on the left. 0-6-2T No 3738 of 1881, a Webb 'Coal Tank' as LMS No 27585, motor-fitted ready to take the 5.45pm down to Holywell Junction on 27 May 1947. *W. A. Camwell*

Below: St Winifred's Halt had an even smaller goods yard really only for coal merchants. The ruling grade being 1:27 all goods trains descended with brakes pinned down. *J. Valentine*

The Llanberis Branch (1869-1964)

This opened as the locally-inspired Carnarvon & Llanberis with Morfa as its starting point. Connected to the Bangor & Carnarvon in 1870 (page 50) it was worked by the L&NW from the beginning. The L&NW's Chairman, Sir Richard Moon attended the opening ceremony. Alas! the mountains did not attract the tourists in the expected droves and business from its three diminutive sidings into a firebrick factory, a slate works and a flannel factory never amounted to anything. A branch over to Betws Garmon never materialised so the valley of the Afon Gwyrfai was left to the North Wales Narrow Gauge and the extension beyond Llanberis was also forgotten.

Above: It was a very lovely journey, a train to Caernarfon is seen near Hafotty drawn by a 2-4-2T of Webb design. *R. G. Williamson*

Below: Llanberis station was a pleasantly-situated little terminus. LMS Fowler 2-6-2T Class 4P No 2366 of 1929 as LMR No 42366 on the 'Carnarvonshire Rail Tour' jointly arranged by the Stephenson Locomotive Society and the Manchester Locomotive Society, 5 May 1957. *J. W. T. House*

The Llandudno Branch (1858-   )

This short branch with the most heavy weekend and bank holiday traffic arose out of the St George's Harbour Act of 1853 Llandudno may have qualified for the award for highest percentage of late arrivals in the country but nobody seemed to mind; it was expected.

Above: Of course one had been seeing the sea to the north of the train for miles and miles but Llandudno Junction was the gateway to the particular boarding house and beach. Seen here in 1898 as newly rebuilt with the L&NW's typical signals with the change-colour spectacles mounted well below the arms.
J. W. P. Arrowsmith in The Railway Magazine

Below: Between the ages of 8 and 12 the author travelled many miles in the back of a narrow four-wheeled BSA car, one of the 200-odd which used up war surplus two-cylinder air-cooled engines no longer required in Avro trainers. There was many a long wait here to the 'tchonka-tchonka, tchonka-tchonka' of those two massive pots. Deganwy with roadway, railway and footway superimposed 1975. *G. H. Platt*

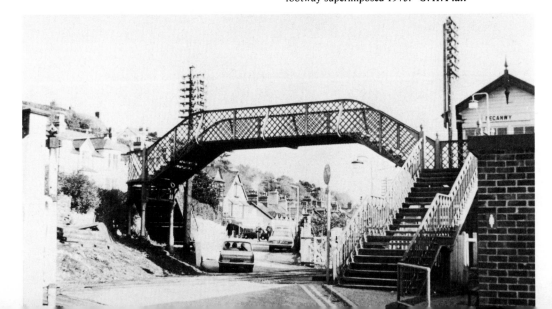

The London & North Western Branches across Clwyd

Rhyl to Corwen (1864-1953/1968)

The line was built in two stages. The Vale of Clwyd was built by David Davies who was later to go on to build much of the Cambrian. He was credited with working a 16 hour day and sleeping on cold nights with his legs inside the cooling firebox of the engine. Then came the Denbigh, Ruthin & Corwen. A Great Western attempt to buy in this spur to the North Wales coast failed and the L&NW secured both companies. Closure was effected in several stages.

Above: Originally the Vale of Clwyd had its northern terminus on Foryd Pier on the opposite side of the river from Rhyl seen in 1956. *J. M. Dunn*

Left: Ruthin had a medium-sized station and a goods yard large enough to cope with a good local traffic. BR Standard class 2-6-4T No 80086 of 1954 on the 9am from Chester, 22 April 1955. *W. A. Camwell*

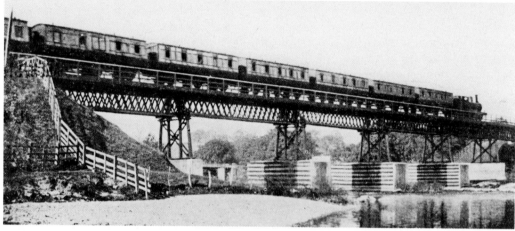

Top: One of the LMS's repeats of the 'Crimson Ramblers'; the beautiful Midland Deeley compounds. Class 4P No 1093 of 1925 on the 4.12pm Rhyl-Denbigh at Trefnant on 27 May 1947. *W. A. Camwell*

Above: To approach the GW-operated Vale of **Llangollen** the line had to be taken across the Dee. This early bridge based on lattice and slender tubes was already in trouble when this picture was taken and had to be replaced later. *Courtesy of R. M. Platt*

Below: Back to the Webb look again. 2-4-2T No 1378 of 1897 as LMS No 6748, just arrived in Corwen with the 3.45pm ex-Denbigh on 24 May 1947. *W. A. Camwell*

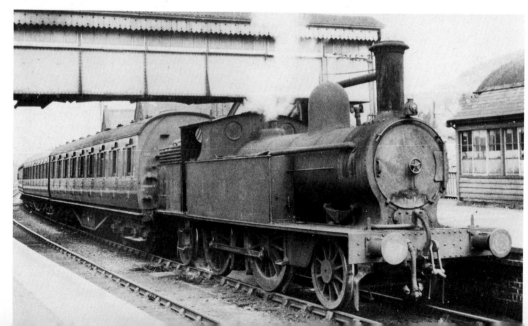

Saltney Ferry (Junction) to Denbigh (1869-1965)

The Mold Railway was opened in 1849 run by the Chester & Holyhead. By its mineral branches the riches of Clwyd had been tapped and extension further west was of little importance.

Thus the Mold & Denbigh Junction became the late starter of 1869; and as an independent legal entity it became a very late finisher. Originally the L&NW had tried to reach the county town of Denbigh by promising to construct the line. Having soon after secured the Vale of Clwyd it obstructively failed to construct. When defeated by the appointment of an independent contractor Sir Richard Moon connived with the Chairman of the House of Lords Committee to have the running powers between Trefnant and Denbigh declared inoperative; so forcing the hard-pressed little company to build over a mile of duplicated embankment which was never used to reach Denbigh. The nearly-bankrupt company had then to agree to ruinous terms for operation by the L&NW as increased costs and litigation had soaked up all the funds needed to buy locos and stock. Even the LMS saw no reason for reducing the profit from working the line by acquiring the company and the poor little thing eked out its penurious existence until BR put it out of its misery in 1948.

Great Britain was, in mid-Victorian times, self-supporting in mineral greases and lubricating oils; and by Young's patent process the burning oil now called paraffin. All were obtained by the distillation of cannel coal of which there were rich seams round Coed Talwrn and Padeswood. The fatal casks of paraffin at Abergele in the 1868 wreck of the 'Irish Mail' probably came from here. This thriving industry was killed off by imports; the first Pennsylvanian gusher roared in 1859 when the first locos for the Llanidloes & Newton Railway were being dragged across Wales by horse and cart. (*Cambrian Railways Album* page 12). By 1883 we were getting Russian oil. Further, the incandescant gas mantle had ruined the sale of wick-fed oil lamps, and over the years the price of paraffin had plummeted from 3/6 (17p) per gallon to 4d (1½p), barrels free. So even the Mold Railway was in for a long twilight of local-only usage. After the formal final closure a spasmodic goods service to Rhydymwyn was restarted in 1974; via the line near Hope Exchange.

Left: Believed to be a seaside outing of the Leeswood Oil Works' employees and their families awaiting their special train at Coed Talon station.
Clwyd Record Office

65

Right: Ironical sighting, a BR Class 25 on a short train of tank wagons passing the site of Padeswood station in 1976. Obviously not a local product. *G. H. Platt*

Below: At Hope & Penyffordd, another product of 'Midlandisation', a Johnson design of Class 2P 4-4-0 No 671 of 1932 as LMR No M671 on the 2.25pm Corwen-Chester, 10 July 1948. *W. A. Camwell*

Bottom: Nine years later, LMS Fowler 2-6-2T Class 3P No 15559 of 1931 as LMR No 40060 on the 12.46pm Denbigh-Chester. *W. A. Camwell*

Top: Yet another thoroughly reliable Midland design continued under grouping. 0-6-0 Fowler 'Big Goods' Class 4F No 4493 of 1927 as LMR No 44493 leaving Bodfari on the daily pickup goods February 1958. *J. I. C. Boyd*

Above: At Denbigh when a train stood already at the north end of the platform a fresh arrival from the north had to pass via the loop and set back to the platform. Webb 2-4-2T No 2126 of 1893 as LMS No 6650 has just reversed to 'unload' the 10.40pm Chester-Corwen, 26 May 1947. *W. A. Camwell*

Left: Denbigh shed in 1947 has a mainly Webb look but there is one outsider, a Midland Johnson Class 3F 0-6-0. *W. Potter*

The Joint Route to Wrexham (1872-1963)

The Ffrith and Tryddyn branches off the Mold Railway had formed the Coed Talon triangle and had connected the cannel collieries, the Coppa, The Nercuis (over a bit of its own private Nerquis Railway) the North Wales and their oil works by 1869.

By 1872 the Ffrith branch had reached Llanfynydd meeting the two miles plus of the GW & L&NW Wrexham and Minera Joint Railway up from the GW at Brymbo. The right of way to Wrexham was complete.

Above: 0-6-2 Webb 'Coal Tank' No 2454 of 1886 as LMS No 7730 on the joint line by Halcog about to enter on to GW metals in the 1920s.
Geoffrey Charles, The National Library of Wales

Right: Demise of the connection to Coed Talon; lifting near Mold-Tryddyn Junction. The original line from Padeswood went in 1934 when the badly-maintained track spread and despatched most of a goods train down an embankment. LMS 0-6-0 Fowler Class 4F No 4389 of 1926 as LMR No 44389 November 1964.
J. I. C. Boyd

The Industrial Branches

These are small branches or yards worked by the owner's engines. In North East Wales they were nearly all standard gauge and ran no regular passenger services. In North West Wales they were nearly all narrow gauge; many had shareholders recruited mainly from the potential users, and could be running regular advertised public passenger services. For convenience of reference these last have been separated under 'Narrow Gauge'.

Here we shall find the most diverse and most interesting examples of the best private engine makers' own designs.

Private Owner Engines

Left: The variety of engines that were to be found at the Brymbo Steel Works makes a good starting point. *Gwynedd* was a massive-looking Black, Hawthorn & Co saddle tank, Works No 1014 of 1890, seen 24 April 1949. *C. P. Knight*

Below: The top-heavy silhouette of *Basic* made her very easy to find. Built by Dubs & Co in 1884, Works No 2064. *Frank Jones*

Above: *Wrekin* was a Fox, Walker & Co engine, their Works No 291 of 1876. Here she is as heavily rebuilt, June 1955. *Frank Jones*

Below:But who on earth would have recognised her as she was built?
The Geoffrey Charles Collection, the National Library of Wales

Left: Sometimes modellers design their models from imaginary scenarios. But if someone said his loco was made out of an old coal wagon, cog-driven through the floor by an agricultural engine; and that the boiler and firebox were unsafe so a vertical boiler had been stuck on at one end as a substitute he would be the subject of a few funny remarks. However that is just what *Express* was. She was put together (rather than built) by a Mr William Lea in 1874 at the Coed Talon Colliery and she was probably worked until 1910 when the pit closed. *F. Lea in The Railway Magazine*

Below: At the Broughton & Plas Power Coal Co's Bersham Colliery we see something much more modern. Andrew Barclay, Sons & Co built their No 1831 in 1924. Seen 30 August 1948. *L. W. Perkins*

Bottom: Of similar period was Llay Main Colliery's *David* from the Avonside Engine Co Ltd. Works No 1868 of 1921. The notice above the cylinder warns ANY PERSON FOUND TAKING COAL FROM LOCO BUNKERS WILL BE SEVERELY DEALT WITH BY ORDER. There is nothing new about 'perks'. Taken in June 1955. *Frank Jones*

Above: Roberts & Maginnis Ltd had *F. W. Cooper*, a little Manning Wardle engine at their silica brick works at Trefor . *R. G. Pratt*

Below: Manning Wardle & Co Ltd's products had a high reputation for standing up to the rough work imposed upon them by railway contractors and many found their way on to the rails they had built; or into private use. *Henrietta* on the Minera Lead Co's steep line had an extra feature. The tall cylinder carrying the safety valves probably houses also the steam feed to the regulator to stop her spraying boiling water all over the landscape as she worked facing uphill. Seen c1890 she went later to the Hundred of Manhood & Selsey as their *Sidlesham*. *Clwyd Record Office*

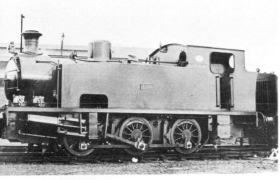

Above: *Arkayar* too has received a bit of makeshift attention. The cab is planking and corrugated iron and the chimney is stovepipe. New in 1888 she was built at Hudswell Clarke & Co's Railway Foundry Works No 303. Seen at the Partington Iron and Steel Co's casting-sand pits at Bodfari in 1929. *Arkayar* was so named from the initials of the first owner Mr R. K. Roberts who owned a bleach works at Tottington near Bury. *R. G. Pratt*

Centre left: By comparison the fleet at John Summers & Sons Ltd's Hawarden Bridge Steel Works (across the Dee but belonging economically and socially to Shotton) finished with some splendid-looking engines. *Titan*, Hudswell Clarke Works No 1820 of 1949 worked alas only 15 years before scrapping. *L. W. Perkins*

Bottom left: Cudworth & Johnson Ltd, Locomotive Dealers, Eagle Foundry, Wrexham, were a sort of latterday Isaac Watt Boulton. Anything that would work and much that wouldn't was bought, overhauled and resold. Also they had a large fleet on hire and maintenance. *Swansea*, built by the Hunslet Engine Co Ltd No 648 of 1897, was one of these. Seen, plus planking and peepholes working (or resting) for W. Y. Craig & Sons Ltd's Ifton Colliery off the GW's Shrewsbury-Chester line in 1940; before Cudworth & Johnson took it on. *W. A. Camwell*

Private Owner Wagons

One could present the commercial history of an area with pictures of all the private owner wagons had they all come to light and if we had enough space. A few will have to do.

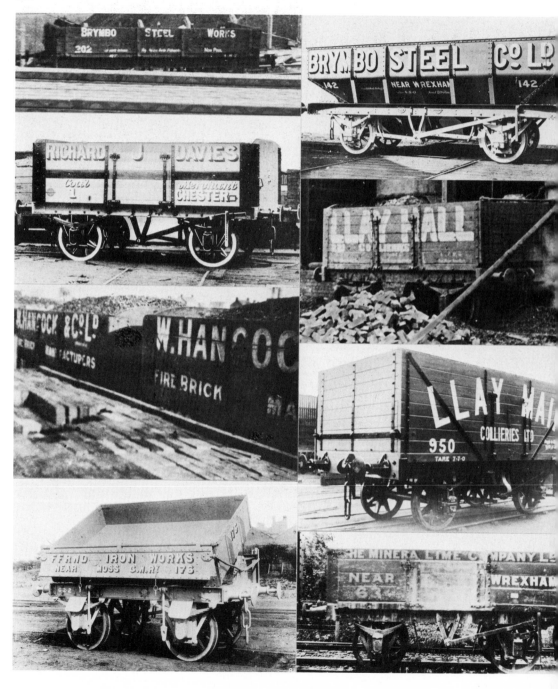

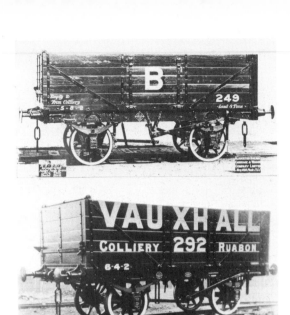

Colliery wagons such as Llay Main, Vauxhall, Vron, Westminster and Wynn Hall could range far and wide as could those of the larger collection/delivery merchants like Ruabon who were 'Coal Merchants to Her Majesty and the Royal Family'. Richard J. Davies sent his wagons to the collieries to collect. Mineral working is exampled by Minera Lime and John & James Stoddard. Iron and steel are represented by Ffrwd Iron and the Brymbos and lastly we see W. Hancock for the 'brikils'. There are others on pages 16, 29 and 72.

Acknowledgements — Minera and Ruabon — J. P. Richards; Davies, Ffrwd and Stoddard — courtesy of R. S. Carpenter; Brymbo open — R. W. Miller; Hancock — Clwyd Record Office; Remainder — The Historical Model Railway Society.

Industrial Branches at Work

Geography, success or management parsimony had such effects that one could not possibly imagine what one was going to see when visiting for the first time.

Above: In 1872 Dundas was declared bankrupt and had to sell the Aston Hall Colliery but he retained toll rights over the tramway (page 13) and had to be consulted in 1877 'to settle the locomotive line'. It looks however as if his bust was still in the yard in the 1890s, a queer thing to see by modern standards. Also of note is the steam boiler outdoors while the beam engine driving the winding gear is fully housed. The 'Locomotive Line' is in the foreground and then it was known as The Aston Branch Railway. *Clwyd Record Office*

Right: The great Westminster Colliery horse-marshalled its own yard and one of the GW's midget 0-4-0STs returned the empties and collected the loaded wagons. No 15 once Shrewsbury & Chester No 15 built by Bury, Curtis & Kennedy in 1847 is the duty engine and a three horse team is hitched to six wagons in the background. *Clywd Record Office*

Left: Kinmel Camp Military Railway had been laid down during World War 1 and the track was taken over by St George's Limeworks. *Eleanor*, Avonside Engine Co 1432 of 1902 eases her train over a level crossing on 30 March 1951. *J. I. C. Boyd*

Below left: The internal railway at the Whitehaven Works, Porthywaen (page 20) was 4ft gauge until 1951. No 1, built by W. J. Bagnall Ltd their No 2466 of 1932 is moving lump stone to the crushers. *J. I. C. Boyd*

Below: Another mid-winter scene with the front of the engine encased in rime. *Olwen*, Beyer, Peacock & Co Ltd's No 5408 of 1910 shunts modern hopper wagons at Lythgoe Bros Ltd's Minera Limestone Quarry in 1963. *J. I. C. Boyd*

Bottom: Sharp curves, uneven track, chunks of coal underfoot, a restless saddle tank; no other picture has captured the colliery scene better. *Shakespeare*, an 0-4-0ST from R & W Hawthorn, Leslie & Co Ltd, No 3072 of 1914 at Bersham Colliery, one of the very few in North Wales to stay working under the National Coal Board, 21 August 1973. *Tom Heavyside*

The Industrial Railway Horse

The horse was for very many years a very active factor in moving both minerals and finished goods on to the steam railways. Generally shunting horses would be large Clydesdales or Shires.

Above: In the Minera Limestone Quarry an extensive fan of narrow gauge rails fed the broken stone to the crushers. *Clwyd Record Office*

Centre right: McDougall of 'Self Raising Flour' fame used a 2ft gauge tramway to carry materials for his Fairbourne seaside venture from a siding off the Cambrian. He also ran a passenger service and here it can be seen that where there was room a horse working on a narrow gauge line usually pulled by walking alongside the track rather than between the rails. *Courtesy of E. W. Hannan*

Bottom right: Hancocks' Lane End Brickworks kept their end of the 3ft 6in tramways until the 1930s reaching the tranship wharf through a curving tunnel. Track was a rare mixture, bullhead laid flat, early edge rail and earlier tramplate and channel castings. Three generations of wheels, unflanged, double flanged and single flanged have been found. Latterly the shipping boxes of the 1860s were used simply as trucks with single-flanged wheels. Mr Alec Hughes with Sam who looks like a Vanner. *Courtesy of Alec Hughes*

78

Above: The GW ran the Wrexham & Minera branch past the Cae-llo Brick Works in 1862. Exactly 100 years later the clay was still being got to the works by horsepower along the original course of the 50cm tramway. This horse doesn't seem to care where he walks. *M. E. M. Lloyd*

Below: Where the railways left off horses took over and the 1900s saw the prime of the heavy road horse. The advent of the hard roadway had induced the construction of vehicles having wheels smaller than those on the traditional great wains. The lower draft angle so needed for carting was got usually by crossing Shire and

Percheron and sometimes there would be a dash of Welsh Cob. This produced a powerful yet more compact animal and the Percheron ancestry led to less of the dense mud-collecting leg hair and they became known as Shire Types or Vanners. These teams were marvels that were disappearing when the author was a boy. There were great snorts of steam as they clomped by on a cold day; the lead horse was checked when the front of the cart was past the gateway, then it was brought back turning the whole team upon itself in a great heaving U, then the U became an S and the whole shouting panting rattling entourage would roll cleanly through the gate into the yard. At St Asaph c1890 with a nine ton boiler. *Clwyd Record Office*

The Manchester & Milford (1867-1965)

This company's grandiose first project, a diagonal route connecting Central Wales to the coast and to South Wales became 'the branch line that never was'. It stirred first in 1845, had a 7ft gauge hiccup in 1854, completed Railway No 1 in 1864 and performed some over-optimistic works towards Railway No 2. Unlike the GW over the Bala & Festiniog it listened to good advice and realised that it was building a loss-leader.

Above: The Debateable Land — Agreement could not be reached over the construction of Penpontbren Junction. Mr Eric Hannan stands on the left at the start of Mid Wales ground, Mrs Edith Hannan on the right marks Manchester & Milford ground. The camera is over Mid Wales ground from Llanidloes. In the end the Llanidloes & Newtown was called in to construct the track and the junction.

Below left: The Bridge where Trainspotters wait in vain. Only one token train was run by the contractor in 1864.

Below right: End of Track — Railway No 1 ended in this shallow cutting above Llangurig. The line was declared officially open to enable the Cambrian to sting the Manchester & Milford for the useless facilities at Llanidloes.

Above left: Costly Cutting — Track was being taken up for re-use by 1882 but when a horse fell down the bank and broke its leg the company was made to fence the lot.

Above right: Relic — Cast iron straining posts made by The Iron Wire Fence Co 2 Poets Corner can still be seen and may date from this event.

Below left: The Bridge that never bore a Train — All the works above the main road to Aberystwyth are the anticipatory efforts towards Railway No 2.

Below right: The Tunnel that was never built — The author's rucksack and camera bag lie on the floor of the pilot cutting above Nant Ceiliog.

Bottom left: The other side of the Mountain — The Myherin Gorge where from the right (as marked by rucksack and camera bag) the trains would have burst out of the $1\frac{1}{4}$ mile tunnel and across the infant Myherin going to Devil's Bridge and on to Aberystwyth thereby robbing us of the delightful narrow gauge Vale of Rheidol Railway.

Bottom right: The Myherin Cutting is harder to find than the Nant Ceiliog; there was a considerable earthfall and trees were planted right on the fall in 1945.
All C. C. Green

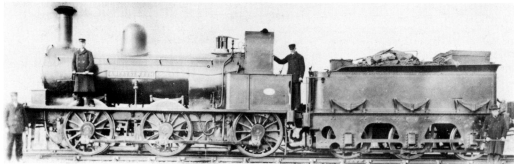

Top: The consolation prize, the part between Aberystwyth and Pencader Junction looked, when running, remarkably like the Cambrian. Driver Edward Benbow was very proud of his smart black engine with its orange lining, new from Sharp, Stewart & Co in 1866 (No 1305). No 3 *Lady Elizabeth* lasted right through until the GW took over in 1906. Benbow once took the cutting down to Aberystwyth Harbour too fast and the resulting hollow in the profile was dubbed Twll Benbow (Benbow's Hole).

Above: No 4 *Aberystwyth* came from Manning Wardle & Co Ltd and maybe they should have stuck to saddle tanks (page 72). Starting with cracked spokes and other defects she was known derisively as 'The Old Boat'. Driver 'Peg' Davies is by the smokebox and on the footplate is his stammering fireman 'Dai Tio'. *Courtesy of Mrs Maggie Owen*

Below: The GW put steam rail cars on the light local service. This picture was taken to record the Rheidol floods on 16 July 1909. *Courtesy of J. G. Rees*

Above: Later any of the smaller Dean engines could be seen with a nice old mixture of coaches. This 4-4-0, once an 0-4-4 broad gauge saddle tank conveys four odd coaches and four horse boxes. Just along here a young newly-passed fireman had the fright of his life; he found himself alone on the footplate. He looked back along the train but there was no crumpled little form in faded blue overalls lying on the ballast. He looked along both sides of the engine and on top of the tender, nothing; then, just as he was realising that he was in charge and wondering what to do a head bobbed round the side of the smokebox. His driver was Jack Bach, one of the great characters of Aberystwyth shed and the only man allowed to carry his own little box from engine to engine to stand on so that he could see through the cab spectacles. He had learned his craft on the chancy

Davies & Metcalfe engines on the Vale of Rheidol and unless extra oil was liberally sloshed on the crosshead guides at stops they would hot up. He thought one of Mr Dean's engines might need the same help and had been oiling the motion while running.
Courtesy of Selwyn Higgins

Below: Royal visits to Wales usually included ceremonial in both and the North and the South; and the M&M was usually part of the Royal route. On 8 August 1955 in between engagements in South Wales, Her Majesty The Queen accompanied by Prince Philip opened the Welsh Plant Breeding Station at Gogerddan near Aberystwyth. LMS Class 8F 2-8-0 Nos 48309 of 1943 and 48707 of 1944 racing the Royal train up the bank near Trawscoed after leaving Aberystwyth at 11.05pm. *Ifor Higgon*

The Narrow Gauge Branches

Simple economics dictated that such things should exist. The cutting of a ledge round a hillside could cost four times as much in standard gauge as in narrow; and the bare weights of metal for an engine alone was much in the same ratio. A narrow gauge line might just be nursed in to a state of labour-intensive workability under conditions which forbade the expense of the larger module. Most of them were primarily mineral lines and did their jobs extremely well for many years except where initial geological surveys were at fault and mines failed prematurely.

The Corris Railway (Horse 1859 — Loco 1879-1948)

The charmingly-named Corris, Machynlleth & River Dovey Tramroad brought slate to the tiny port of Cei Ward near Derwenlas. After only eight years the standard gauge arrived and scooped up the slate trade via exchange sidings at Machynlleth and the sailing ships were abandoned to rot away.

Right: North of Corris lay several quarries and the Ratgoed Tramway and slate had to be brought through the diminutive passenger station. No 3 Hughes No 323 of 1878 (now on the Talyllyn) 6 July 1936. *S. W. Baker*

Below right: The GW acquired the line with some bus services in 1930 and promptly stopped carrying passengers; but that was not to be the end of it. The make-up of this train is five trucks of coal, four people sitting admiring the sunny scene in two trucks, while another carries their luggage c1934. *F. E. Hemming*

The Festiniog Railway (Horse 1836 — Loco 1863-1946 & 1955-   )

This archtype of narrow gauge steam-hauled mountain railways owes its excellence and success to a Yorkshire surveyor's holiday in Wales and to a chance meeting on the Nantlle Tramway between a quarry owner and an Irish gentleman who lacked an occupation. After his holiday James Spooner had justifiably fallen in love with Wales, and stayed there to work, and it was Samuel Holland on a business trip who met Henry Archer in that tram to Caernarfon. So Henry Archer was given the job of promoting the railway and he was convinced that the local surveyor was also a natural engineer and persuaded James Spooner to accept the appointment. Basically the task was to emulate the successful tramways already working from Dinorwic, Bethesda and Nantlle through far more difficult terrain.

James Spooner's natural flair was transmitted down to his son Charles and he gave the line a track of better quality than many a standard gauge line ever had. When steam operation commenced the gauge was settled at 1ft $11\frac{1}{2}$in which was very close to 60cm (1ft $11\frac{5}{8}$in) much advocated on the continent after France had gone compulsorily metric in 1801.

After the Aberystwyth and Welsh Coast line was completed into Portmadoc an extensive yard and exchange sidings were built at Minffordd. Now coal and other commodities came into the area served by the Festiniog via the standard gauge instead of by sea and much slate was transhipped there on to the standard gauge. So the Cambrian succeeded in winning probably more of the slate traffic out of Festiniog than either the GW or the L&NW ever managed with all their excessive expenditure; but of course the quarry-owning shareholders of the Festiniog had been placated by the use of some 10 miles of their little pet. Gravity working never entirely ceased until c1940.

Above: So the Festiniog Railway's main business was slates and this picture sums it up nicely. The old triangle junction at Dinas in 1887 with an up train propelled by *Palmerston* or *Little Giant*. The special wagons evidence the slates and the materials required are in the remaining vehicles, gunpowder, coal and timber. And in the distance is the haze of slate-dust from the mill. *F. Moore*

Above: Wornout journalistic cliches are no new things. Just as every pensioners' party today is a 'knees-up' so every narrow gauge line was 'A Toy Railway' from the 1890s to around 1925. This nice little picture of *Welsh Pony* at Dinas Terminus was taken from a hand-coloured lantern slide in an excellent set called 'Picturesque Wales' put out by the famous postcard firm. It was No 17 'The Toy Railway'. *J. Valentine*

Below: The other engine type to be looked for along the Traeth Mawr was the celebrated 'Double Fairlie' running on two steam bogies. All firing was done into a pair of back-to-back fireboxes opening to the same side and the driver's controls are on the other side so they only see each others heads when running. No 10 *Merddyn Emrys* was the first engine they built themselves in Boston Lodge works in 1879 seen here in the 1930s. *G. H. W. Clifford*

Above: On a fine day there was much competition for the novelty of sitting in one of the old observation coaches but the return journey in the rain often saw the more comfortable bogie coaches full to capacity.
G. H. W. Clifford

Below: In 1923 joint working with the Welsh Highland Railway came into being under a Light Railway Order. No 1 *Princess* returning to Boston Lodge at the end of the day past the old slate quays. In 1934 the old tracks, points and turntables were still to be seen in roads and pavements about the harbour. *F. E. Hemming*

Top right: On the next day Frank Hemming and his fiancee Evelyn wished to take the train to Duffws using also a ticket for a bicycle. In no way could the staff get their brand-new tandem to fit into carriage or van. So a bogie truck was hitched on at the back and the couple were adjured to keep an eye on it as they travelled and to let the guard know if it became detached. Would it have stayed on all the way down? We shall never know. Traversing Cei Mawr on that journey. *F. E. Hemming*

Centre right: The Snowdon Mountain Tramroad & Hotel Company (page 102) issued a set of picture cards from paintings, including this fanciful effort depicting the Festiniog's route along Llyn Tan-y-bwlch. The engine looks like something out of a painting by Monet. *Collection, C. C. Green*

Below: Will it ever run again? *Palmerston* accumulating rust at Boston Lodge Works 23 July 1951. The gentleman is Mr Robert Evans, the Company's last general manager; but, as they used to write in the contemporary magazines of the Festiniog's first heyday **'Peruse on, gentle reader'.** *R. C. Riley*

The Glyn Valley Tramway (Horse 1873 — Loco 1891-1935)

Starting with a gauge of 2ft 4¼in it connected slate, granite and limestone quarries to the GW and to the canal at Chirkbank. There were also wool and flannel mills. By 1887 an improved route over the hitherto forbidden Chirk Castle Estate was cut through to a site west of Chirk station; and the line settled down to the principal business of carrying stone plus a popular but lightly-used passenger service, on a gauge of 2ft 4½in.

Top left: Most of the track was in or alongside road and the locomotives looked a bit like street tram engines; this was what made the line so different. 0-4-2T *Sir Theodore* came from Beyer, Peacock & Co Ltd, their No 2969 of 1888. Seen here when little if any over two years old. *M. D. England Collection, The National Railway Museum*

Centre left: Mixed trains were frequently to be seen. *Glyn*, Beyer, Peacock No 3500 of 1892 at Glyn Ceriog c1895. *F. Moore*

Below: Originally the open carriages were extremely open but had curtains against the weather. By 1895 this flimsy protection seems to have disappeared but later they did receive ends to roof level. From a 3¼in square slide. *Clwyd Record Office*

Interesting Minors

Top left: Solomon Andrews used a 2ft gauge horse-drawn tramway from Barmouth Junction to build Jubilee Terrace; the first and only portion of his projected holiday estate. An ex-Cardiff tram body conveyed passengers and another was the waiting room.
Courtesy of E. W. Hannan

Centre left: The Buckley brikils and collieries used tramway-style chairs of an unusual material along their private branches — hard heavy silica brick. Depicted is part of the branch down from Knowl Hill Brickworks.
C. C. Green

Below left: The Gorseddau Tramway has left this imposing monument up in the mountains where the line curves in below the quarry. It stabilised a loose formation and protected horse and driver from fallings. Gauge was 3ft and the quarry worked c1856-c1875.
John W. Burman

Bottom left: The Hendre-ddu Tramway (1ft 11in gauge c1868-1939) put slates, slab and timber on to the Mawddwy Branch (page 17) at Aberangell. Originally worked by horse and latterly by Simplex Tractor as seen here at the transhipment siding.
Courtesy of David Roberts and Lewis Cozens

Below: The Kerry Tramway (2ft gauge 1888-1895) was the private timber carrier from C. J. Naylor's Bryn Llyarch estate to Kerry (page 15). Some slab was brought down part-way via a horse-drawn upper section with a reversing stage. Bagnall 0-4-2 wing tank No 970 of 1888 was sold and worked later on the construction of the Lynton & Barnstaple as seen here. The line was revived c1917-c1923 for timber.
Courtesy of L. T. George

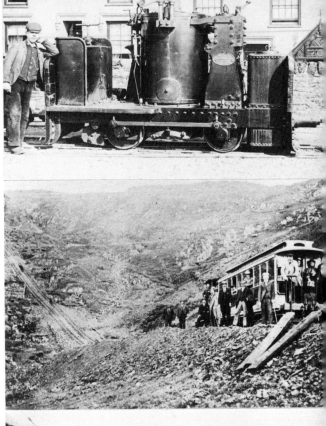

Top right: The Moel-y-gest Tramway (1902-1906) used a part of the Croesor Tramway's old line in Portmadoc. When this Falcon engine had to work over Festiniog metals that company's stationmaster became very worried over what he considered the reckless speed at which this odd-looking loco was being driven.
F. Moore

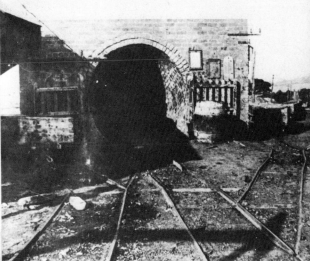

Centre right: The Plynlimon & Hafan Tramway (Gauge 2ft 3in 1897-1899) owed the shortness of its life to geological misjudgment (the setts were said to have been too 'soft'), to land cost wrangling and to the Cambrian's transhipment charges at Llanvihangel (or Llandre). The engine went to the Vale of Rheidol after re-gauging and the coach became a summer house at Llanbadarn.
The National Library of Wales

Below right: The Tan-llan mine was extended as a drift mine with an adit descending gently from ground level via a weather portal. Such tramways inclining into the nether regions were aptly known as 'Pluto Tracks'.
Clwyd Record Office

Below: The Llanymynech limestone tramways ran via inclines down to the newly-extended navigable waters of the canal after 1805. One group ended in a neat little complex of loops and sidings alongside a specially-built basin. The Oswestry & Newtown Railway's original Llanfyllin Branch bridged over the final run and took all the traffic via a diversion line into Rock Siding after 1861. *C. C. Green*

Bottom right: The Trevor Limestone tramway (c1797-c1900?) ended with a long incline down to the bank of the Ellesmere and Llangollen canal by the Sun Inn. When the incline was not working boats were loaded from heaps of stone stockpiled at the bottom as is being done here c1885. The GW Ruabon Branch is to the left of the picture and the canal maintained superiority by bursting and washing the upstart away. *Clwyd Record Office*

The Nantlle Tramway (1828-1872)

This long-lived 3ft 6in gauge line ran originally from the Gloddfarlon Quarries to a quay at Caernarvon. Passengers were carried. The L&NW's Carnarvonshire Railway took its place firstly to Penygroes and by 1872 to Tal-y-sarn (page 51) leaving only 1½ miles at the upper end undisturbed. Although owned by both L&NW and by the LMS it remained horse-drawn to the end (1963) by private contract.

Above: A coal train heading back to the quarries headed by both privately-owned 'industrial locomotives', *Queen* (white livery) and *Prince* (dark livery). *W. A. Camwell*

Below: The principles of working light irregularly-laid tramways — fixed axles and double-flanged wheels with the 3in of slop either way permitting the gauge to vary between 3ft 3in and 3ft 9in, June 1952. *J. T. Clewley*

Top right: The internal 2ft gauge lines in the quarries had to be better-laid. Wagons might be double-flanged but the locos were not. Bagnall 0-4-0ST 2901 of 1919 *Wendy* of the Dorothea Quarry had a big sensible cab. August 1942. *Norman Glover*

Centre right: Pen-yr-orsedd had de Wintons, Hunslets and a Kerr Stuart and pylons carried a Clarke Chapman 'Blondin' system which whisked wagons about overhead as well. *Una* on the left was Hunslet 873 of 1905 and old Pendyffryn dated from 1894. Seen on 18 June 1942. *L. W. Perkins*

Bottom right: Pen-yr-orsedd had one great rarity. Most de Wintons were unsprung ankle-sprainers and one or two are known to have been sprung at the driver's end only but *Arthur* built in 1895 was fully sprung. *W. H. Whitworth*

The North Wales Narrow Gauge Railways (1877-1923) & The Welsh Highland Railway (1923-1936)

The great dream of a narrow gauge main line traversing Wales from Porth Dinllaen in the west to Corwen in the east was scotched by the L&NW (page 56). Reality was confined to a short but well-used branch to the quarries at Bryngwyn and a longer and less thriving arm up to Rydd-ddu near Snowdon. As in other instances once mineral traffic had ceased the line could not be kept profitable. 'Goods as required' trains did run between 1916 and 1922. Under a Light Railway Order the Welsh Highland venture connected to Portmadoc via the defunct Portmadoc, Beddgelert & South Snowdon formations and to the Festiniog via a bit of the old Croesor Tramway. All failed, the postwar tourists were already becoming used to the motor-charabanc, and, worse still, to the private motor car.

Above: A scene at Dinas Junction in 1892, all three engines are ready to take most of the carriage stock to Rhydd-ddu in one long train. *Symons of Llanberis*

Below left: *Gowrie* was bought for a proposed extension to Portmadoc. He (not she) was Hunslet 0-6-4T 979 of 1908, a not too successful single Fairlie, and possibly the last ever to be built. Dinas Junction in 1909. *G. M. Perkins*

Below right: An extension of the dream; had the Ruthin & Cerrig-y-drudion Railway been completed NWNGR stock could have reached Ruthin without a break in gauge. Continuous trackbed stopped here at Buarthau but isolated easy bits were cut further on. The organiser was a fly merchant and the shareholders were glad to buy out his contract of service for £500 to get him off their backs.

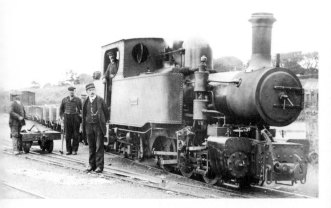

Top: A little girl poses in front of a Festiniog Fairlie at Beddgelert on a very damp day c1924. The Festiniog soon stopped Fairlies going to foreign parts and such pictures are quite rare. *Courtesy of M. E. M. Lloyd*

Above: *Russell*, Hunslet 2-6-2T No 901 of 1906 was a handsome engine bought for the Portmadoc, Beddgelert & South Snowdon. She (he?) was mutiliated by cutting down chimney, dome and cab to try and get through the Festiniog's Moelwyn Tunnel; whence she emerged ignominiously scarred. In the Aberglaslyn Pass 7 August 1933. *Ifor Higgon*

Left: Someone at Frith's thought their card was a touch empty without a train. Mostly the cards on sale were the blank version but a few did come out like this.
F. Frith & Son

95

The Padarn and Penrhyn Railways

They had much in common; both quarries were worked by the gallery system, a series of gigantic steps cut back into the mountains. Both sent their slates to private ports; and to each the L&NW had a short branch with reloading arrangements down on the quays. Both had massive incline systems for getting the slates down to valley level. In details they developed some delightfully interesting differences.

Dinorwic Quarries

Nearly all the engines were 0-4-0 Hunslet saddle tanks named after Assheton-Smith's favourite racehorses and steam yachts. Gauge was 1ft 10¾in.

Above: These little engines spent all their working lives on the high galleries open to the skies. *Red Damsel*, Hunslet 493 of 1889. *Courtesy of E. W. Hannan*

Above right: *Bernstein* and *Maid Marian* back at their tiny shed (probably on Pen-garret), c1,500ft above sea level at the end of the day. *P. J. Lynch*

Right: Where inclines crossed galleries arched ways let the track run through. Where the wagons were finally handled on to the inclines the track was light edge-rail unfit for engines. Note the sharp curve following the easier curve of the point. Engines would push the trains round and halt on the points and thereafter man power took over. *King of the Scarlets*, Hunslet 492 of 1889 on 6 June 1952. *N. Fields*

Penrhyn Quarries

There were Hunslets here too but named after ladies and gentlemen but later second-hand acquisitions were an interesting mixed bag of other makes. The gauge was 1ft 11in.

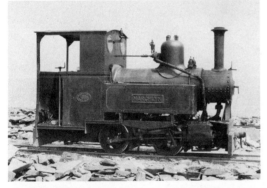

Top left: *Eigiau*, a German engine, Orenstein & Koppel No 5668 of 1912 came from the Dolgarrog Aluminium Corporation in 1929. *Frank Jones*

Left: *Marchlyn* was Avonside Engine Co's 2067 of 1933 and came from Durham County Water Board in 1936. Working here on Twll-dwndwr level 19 June 1942. *Frank Jones*

Below: Eighteen Morris Cowley petrol tractors were specially built at the quarry workshops between 1932 and 1939. 10 July 1934. *P. W. Robinson*

The Padarn Railway (1848-1961)

This 4ft gauge substitute for the 2ft $0\frac{1}{2}$in gauge horse-drawn line of c1824 took a new route along the shore of the lake from which it was named and ended, at the top of an incline down the cliff to the harbour, with a gauge of 1ft $10\frac{3}{4}$in. So the Dinorwic's main line had to be a transporter of narrow gauge wagons.

Above: *Amalthea*, Hunslet 0-6-0T No 410 of 1886 taking two trains to Velinheli (there are two of the four-wheeled guards' hutches) past Pen Llyn Peris 30 June 1961). *Ifor Higgon*

Below: *Amalthea* returning with a double empties train.

Being payday one guard can travel in the pay coach. There were over 20 such coaches, lettered not numbered; they were dropped off in batches at selected points and in the morning the quarrymen returned to the same places for the pickup journey to work. Erw Ffordd on 14 June 1957. *Ifor Higgon*

The Penrhyn Railway (1876-1962)

This too replaced an earlier horse tramway (of 1801) over an improved route. There was no cliff at Port Penrhyn so a well-engineered 1ft 11in gauge main line was the ideal solution. Because of meagre clearances at the port and alongside the L&NW line the extra-powerful engines had their cylinders raised up and tucked in.

Top: *Blanche*, Hunslet 589 of 1893 taking a load of slates and Fullersite from Bethesda to Port Penrhyn on 31 July 1957. Note the guard with his arms folded against the windage. Fullersite was slate dust used as a filler for making terrazzo floors and other forms of dense smooth concrete. Near Felin Hên. *Ifor Higgon*

Above: Return journey with empties and coal at Tregarth loop, *Blanche* again, on 6 October 1959. *Ifor Higgon*

Above: Not trucks of coal but open cars full of be-capped Penrhyn quarrymen going home. *Courtesy of E. W. Hannan*

Below: Once up an engine stayed up and usually only bits that needed repair were sent down, eg a boiler and firebox. Here *Maid Marian* is being let down Dinorwic C1 incline for preservation. Note that the jacks are resting on the front to keep her from lifting. September 1966. *Gordon Ward*

The Pwllheli & Llanbedrog Tramway (1894 & 1896-1928)

Built initially as a contractor's line along the beach for fetching stone to build a seaside resort; the line developed into a popular passenger carrier. Soloman Andrews bought Glyn-y-weddw and installed tearooms, a museum and art gallery and a dance hall and roller-skating rink at the end of a pleasurable three mile ride. Numerous passing loops were provided and several of the 18 or so cars could be weaving round each other at any one time; just as early commerce carriers used to do. Gauge was 3ft

Above: Covered trams at the West End triangular junction. *Wrench Series*

Below: A covered tram waits while the school bus(?) and an umbrella-bearing open car get by.
F. Frith & Co, The National Library of Wales

The Snowdon Mountain Railway (1896-   )

From 1871 vested interests, mountaineers, guides and purist snobs defended the mountain against all attempts to provide an easy way for 'the rabble'. The fatal accident on the first day did cause one death and a lot of cuts and bruises, and two climbers below the falling engine said they thought it was a large boulder they had heard. The Abt rack system was then re-inforced with wing-angles to retain the engine-cogs in mesh with the rack. Gauge was 80cm (2ft 7$\frac{1}{2}$in).

Above: No 4 *Snowdon*, Swiss Locomotive & Machine Works No 988 of 1896 at Clogwyn c1896. *J. Valentine*

Below: The hotel at the top closed at the end of the 1945 summer season. On reading of this a bridegroom anxiously phoned the manager but was assured that his September booking would be all right despite the closure. When the newly wedded couple arrived in Llanberis the weather had broken and the trains had been stopped because of the high winds at the top. 'The carriage might be blown over, but are you Mr and Mrs X? — well now it is all arranged and you are to go up on the engine'. And so they did, driver, fireman, the happy pair and their luggage squashed into the tiny cab and left Llanberis and reached the summit in safety in the howling gale. Thus with a final wonderful gesture the hotel gave shelter to its last guests. Nearing the summit. c1925. *Excel Series*

The Talyllyn Railway (1866-   )

The conveyance of slate from Bryn Eglwys Quarry to the Cambrian at Towyn was the primary reason for building this 2ft 3in gauge line; and it was one of the first to be designed from the start for locomotive working. More passengers came than had been expected and soon extra coaches were bought. All the stock served long and well until a great first was achieved in 1950. The first railway preservation society met in Birmingham and the Talyllyn can claim along with the Windmill Theatre 'We never closed'.

Top left: *Pretoria*, as she was named for a short while, and the A is just visible — taking general goods and empties. Now known by her original name *Dolgoch* she was Fletcher, Jennings & Co's No 63 of 1866.
G. M. Perkins

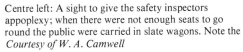

Centre left: A sight to give the safety inspectors appoplexy; when there were not enough seats to go round the public were carried in slate wagons. Note the
Courtesy of W. A. Camwell

Below: After the days work during the early years of the preservation movement. Bill Faulkner is driving the returning train of empties and picks and shovels accompanied by Graham and Mrs 'Gillie' Vincent. The Mercury tractor was of uncertain habits and went backwards like a tortoise and a centre-jack for turning it round was installed underneath. Nowadays we can't have carefree volunteers, the legal eagles raising the question of responsibility have reduced them all to registered unpaid workers. Near Quarry siding 1954.
H. F. Wheeller

The Vale of Rheidol Light Railway (1902-   )

While there was some traffic in lead ore and timber to the Rotfawr wharf and to exchange sidings with both the Manchester & Milford and the Cambrian, trippers were always the main business. It went into standard gauge ownership in 1913 when the Cambrian bought it; then it devolved automatically into the ownerships of the GW and **now to British Rail. Gauge is 1ft 11½in.**

Top: 2-6-2T *Edward VII*, Davies & Metcalfe Ltd No 1 of 1902 in London, Brighton & South Coast colours with varnished pitch-pine coaches all as new.
Lewis The Mart — A. J. Lewis

Above: From 1922 to 1964 the trains were a bright note in the landscape, first in GW livery and later in BR main line colours followed by a return to GW again; all having light upper parts on the coaches. No 8 *Llywelyn* (Swindon-built in 1923) at Rheidol Falls August 1958. *C. C. Green*

Below: 1964 saw the start of the duller period, first a dark green succeeded in 1968 by plain BR rail blue and from a distance the trains are lost in the trees on the mountainsides. On the Aberffrwd curve, No 7 *Owain Glyndŵr* 3 April 1972. *C. C. Green*

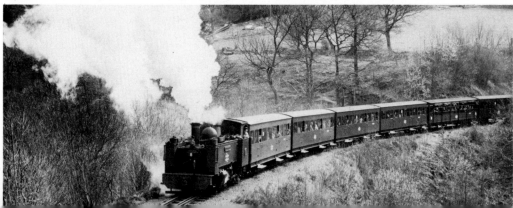

The Welshpool & Llanfair Light Railway (1903-1956 & 1963-   )

'A quiet and peaceful existence connecting the people of Llanfair Caereinion with market town of Welshpool and the Cambrian main line' is an adequate summary of its working days. It was built to 2ft 6in gauge for economy and seemingly even keen photographers overlooked it for years. The Cambrian ran it, the GW stopped its passenger service and BR closed it.

Top left: 0-6-0T *The Earl* (for the Earl of Powys), Beyer, Peacock No 3496 of 1903 and train all in Cambrian livery in Welshpool c1905. The card was not written and posted until 1924; a typical example of the length of time some of these cards lay around in village shops until 20 years ago when the collecting craze took hold. *J. Valentine*

Centre left: An enthusiasts' special drawn by *The Earl* as WR No 822 forms a much longer train than those which plied during the end of commercial working. Much of the line was hidden from the competing road by a high hedge and the author recollects an assembly of copper rim, tip of dome, and top of cab; all only 27ft from a van roof; chuffling quietly to itself behind the hedge. *Ifor Higgon*

Below: The preservation society has acquired a fine collection of fresh locos and stock from overseas and has built an extremely effective works for their maintenance. Basil Roberts is cutting angle for new wagon doors; *Sir Drefaldwyn's* new superheater tubes lie behind her on the left, the Zillertalbahn coach is being replanked, and *Countess* is getting a complete overhaul. Seen on 3 May 1979. *C. C. Green*

Railway Buses

These had but little effect on the railway services of their day but nonetheless they were the 'little cloud out of the sea like a man's hand' which foretold the storm.

Top left: About 1905 the L&NW put on a service between Mold, Flint and Connah's Quay where it already had stations, and so competing with itself albeit avoiding the use of two trains. *Clwyd Record Office*

Bottom left: In 1906 the Cambrian put two Orion buses on between Pwllheli and Nevin; but this was at least an extension of railway services. *Cambrian Official*

Top: The Corris Railway was very enterprising in the matter of extending their tourist attractions beyond the terminus by the use of horse-drawn charabancs. Inevitably these were replaced by motors and we see the two Bristols AE1157 and AE1158 posed on Bwlch-llyn-bach. *George & Son*

Above: In 1919 the Kent brothers sank their gratuities into a pair of ex-WD six-wheelers, a 3ton Thornycroft and a 30cwt Morris to run a summer service from Devils Bridge to the top of Plynlimon. The GW acquired the Morris and promptly advertised the trip as if it had been an inspiration from Paddington. *C. F. H. Kent*

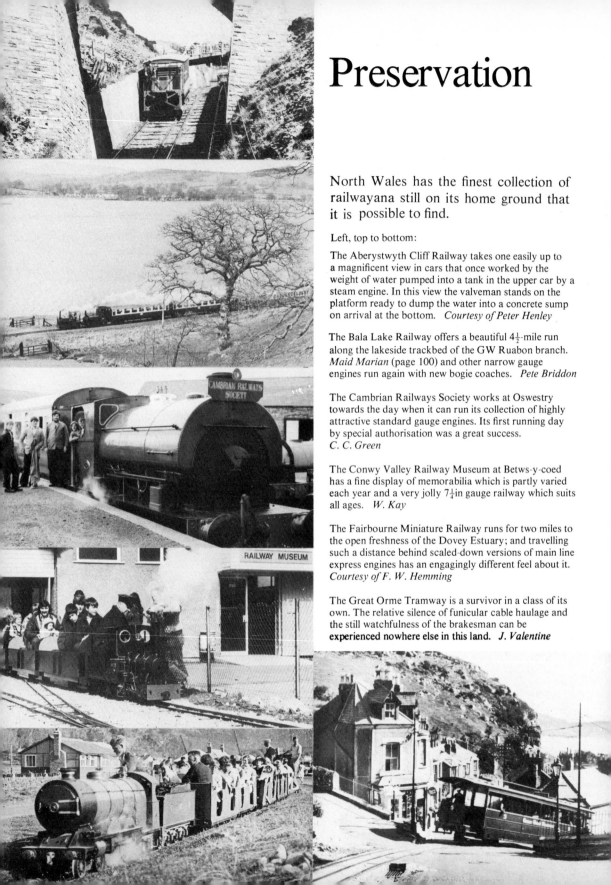

Preservation

North Wales has the finest collection of railwayana still on its home ground that it is possible to find.

Left, top to bottom:

The Aberystwyth Cliff Railway takes one easily up to a magnificent view in cars that once worked by the weight of water pumped into a tank in the upper car by a steam engine. In this view the valveman stands on the platform ready to dump the water into a concrete sump on arrival at the bottom. *Courtesy of Peter Henley*

The Bala Lake Railway offers a beautiful $4\frac{1}{2}$-mile run along the lakeside trackbed of the GW Ruabon branch. *Maid Marian* (page 100) and other narrow gauge engines run again with new bogie coaches. *Pete Briddon*

The Cambrian Railways Society works at Oswestry towards the day when it can run its collection of highly attractive standard gauge engines. Its first running day by special authorisation was a great success. *C. C. Green*

The Conwy Valley Railway Museum at Betws-y-coed has a fine display of memorabilia which is partly varied each year and a very jolly $7\frac{1}{4}$in gauge railway which suits all ages. *W. Kay*

The Fairbourne Miniature Railway runs for two miles to the open freshness of the Dovey Estuary; and travelling such a distance behind scaled-down versions of main line express engines has an engagingly different feel about it. *Courtesy of F. W. Hemming*

The Great Orme Tramway is a survivor in a class of its own. The relative silence of funicular cable haulage and the still watchfulness of the brakesman can be **experienced nowhere else in this land.** *J. Valentine*

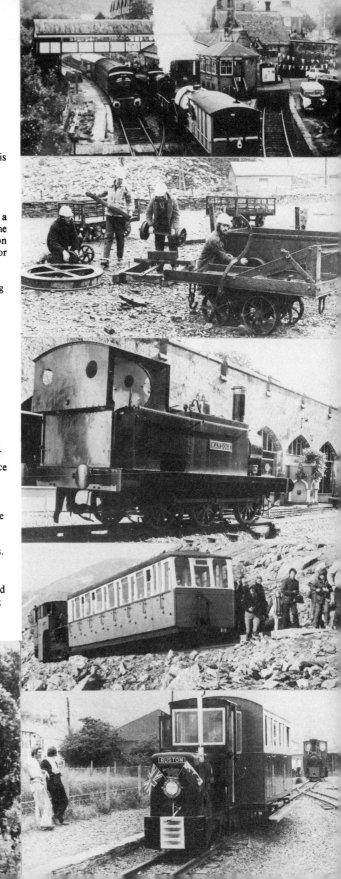

Below: The Llanberis Lake Railway uses nearly two miles of the old Padarn route. Three of the engines worked high on the mountain above Gilfach-ddu which is now an extensive museum of quarrying. *R. Gartside*

Right, top to bottom:

The Llangollen Railway Society have the station as a museum and locos and rolling stock are on display. The objective is to bring to life a section of the Ruabon branch and GW 0-6-0PT No 7754 is there for restoration. *Llangollen Railway Society*

The Llechwedd Caverns Tramway at Blaenau Ffestiniog takes visitors right inside a mountain by miners' train; and much interesting equipment has been restored and put on view. *Llechwedd Caverns*

Penrhyn Castle National Trust Museum is a place to go and spend many happy hours, items in care are so well displayed and so varied. Much of local and railway interest is to be seen in most impressive surroundings. *Creative Photographers*

The Snowdon Mountain Railway remains the unique thing it always was; a European Rack Railway in the Welsh Mountains. The modern belief in greater comfort has been kept in mind and the open carriages beloved of our tougher Victorian great-grandparents have long since been replaced. *J. I. C. Boyd*

The Welsh Highland Railway at Portmadoc battled for 17 years against a dismaying array of receivers, red tape and legalities to win through to their Light Railway Order in 1980. They have *Russell*, one of the original native steam engines (page 95), and three from overseas. The scene shows readiness for a triumphant first run. *C. J. Keylock*

The Corris Railway Society run a museum in Corris and the North Clwyd Railway Association is in active being at Prestatyn to take over the still-existant Prestatyn & **Dyserth Branch.**

Left: The Festiniog Railway runs again to much purpose and at Ddaullt three quarters of the way up there are now striking innovations. The declared ambition has always been to overcome the illicit flooding of the Moelwyn Tunnel by the Central Electricity Generating Board. This achievement is in sight thanks to the perseverance and sheer determination of some very worthy enthusiasts known as 'The Deviationists'. Penrhyn Railway's *Linda* on Rhoslyn Bridge, part of a new Darjeeling-Himalaya style climbing loop which lifts the line some 25ft on to the new route. *N. F. Gurley*

Bottom left: The mountain region in which the deviationists and their girl-friends and wives wrought so much. *Blanche* approaching Tan-y-grisiau past Lyn Ystradau. Now one can buy a through ticket for that marvellous journey between Llandudno and Portmadoc with break of gauge at the new Blaenau Ffestiniog station. *Tom Heavyside*

Top right: The Talyllyn Railway is now extended to Nant Gwernol so the run exceeds seven miles up the gentle fertile valley and along the ledge section at the upper end. Tywyn Wharf houses the society's excellent museum. *J. F. Rimmer*

Centre right: The Vale of Rheidol has a 12-mile scenic run of the highest quality. BR are carefully renovating and repanelling all the coaches and engines are being repainted in historic liveries. A named train has been introduced and the picture shows the inaugural run of the 2.30pm ex-Aberystwyth as the 'Welsh Dragon' with No 8 *Llywelyn* newly repainted in Great Western green arriving at Devil's Bridge on 6 May 1981. *C. C. Green*

Below: The Welshpool & Llanfair Light Railway takes the visitor through eight miles of extremely pretty countryside. Besides the original two engines there is that wonderful collection of overseas specimens all in running order. *F. E. Hemming*

Postscript

Well, there it is, only an epitome; North Wales had so much and so many. We have traced the over-taking of horse-drawn railways by those hauled by steam and we have touched on the eclipse of steam by the diesel. The future of our steam railways lies largely with the preservation societies. They have the enthusiasm; they need the resources. I hope this book will leave its readers with the urge to seek out 'The Great Little Trains of Wales' and their kindred societies and museums. Without the support of many visitors they may still decline and fail; and Wales will have lost irreplaceable attractions.

Ôl-nodyn

Wel, dyna ni, dim ond crynodeb; bu gan Ogledd Cymru y fath gyfoeth, o ran defnyddiau ac o ran dynion. Yr ydym wedi amlinellu hanes disodli'r rheilffyrdd tynnu-gan-geffyl gan y rhai a oedd yn dibynnu ar ager, ac wedi cyffwyrdd â disodli ager gan danwydd diesel. Y mae dyfodol ein rheilffyrdd ager yn dibynnu bron yn gyfan gwbl bellach ar y cymdeithasau cadwraeth. Y mae ganddynt hwy'r brwdfrydedd angenrheidiol, ond y mae angen adnoddau arnynt. Yr wyf yn gobeithio y bydd y llyfr hwn yn symbylu ei ddarllenwyr i fynd i chwilio am 'drenau bychain mawr Cymru' a'r cymdeithasau a'r amgueddfeydd sydd ynglŷn â hwy. Heb gefnogaeth llu o ymwelwyr gallant eto ddihoeni a methu; a byddai hynny'n golygu fod Cymru'n colli atyniadau anhepgor.

Bibliography

Baughan, Peter E.; *Regional History of the Railways of Great Britain Vol II North & Mid Wales*

Bentley, James; Articles in *The Buckley Magazine*

Birmingham Loco Club; Pocketbook F *Industrial & Independent Locomotives & Railways of North Wales*

Bowen, E. G.; *Wales*

Boyd, J. I. C.; *The Festiniog Railway and Narrow Gauge Railways in Mid Wales, in North Caernarvonshire and in South Caernarvonshire*

Castledine, D. C.; *The Ruthin & Cerrigydrudion Railway*

Christiansen, Rex; *Forgotten Railways, North & Mid Wales*

Christiansen & Miller; *The Cambrian Railways* Vols I & II

Cozens, Lewis; Books about the Cambrian Branches

Davies, Glyn; *Minera*

Dean, R. J.; Historical Notes for a Tour of Flintshire Railways

Dow, George; *Great Central* Vols II & III

Dunn, J. M.; Articles in the *Railway Magazine*

Giffard, H. P. W.; *The Former Cannel Oil Industry in North Wales & Staffordshire*

Green, C. C.; *Cambrian Railways Album* and Vol II

Holden, J. S.; *The Manchester & Milford Railway*

Hollingsworth, Brian; *Festiniog Adventure*

Lerry, G. G.; *The Denbighshire Collieries*

McDermot & Clinker; *History of The Great Western Railway*

Morgan, Bryan; *Railway Relics*

Railway Correspondence & Travel Society; The *Locomotives of the Great Western* and others in the series

The Railway Magazine; Various Articles

Thomas, R. D.; *The Industries of the Morda Valley*

Thompson, Trefor; *The Prestatyn & Dyserth Railway*

Wilson, E. A.; *The Ellesmere & Llangollen Canal*

The Wrexham Leader; Articles by Silin